ROBBEN ISLAND

James W. Fish

Robben Island

An account of thirty-four years
of gospel work among
lepers in South Africa

James W. Fish

JOHN RITCHIE LTD
CHRISTIAN PUBLICATIONS

40 Beansburn, Kilmarnock, Scotland

ISBN-13: 978 1 909803 72 5

Copyright © 2013 by John Ritchie Ltd.
40 Beansburn, Kilmarnock, Scotland

www.ritchiechristianmedia.co.uk

All rights reserved. No part of this publication may be reproduced, stored in a retrievable system, or transmitted in any form or by any other means – electronic, mechanical, photocopy, recording or otherwise – without prior permission of the copyright owner.

Typeset by John Ritchie Ltd., Kilmarnock
Printed by Bell & Bain Ltd., Glasgow

CONTENTS.

CHAPTER.		PAGE.
I.	FOREWORD	1
II.	THE EARLY HISTORY OF ROBBEN ISLAND (by G. F. Gresley)	10
III.	THE HISTORY OF LEPROSY	22
IV.	THIRTY-FOUR YEARS' WORK AMONGST THE LEPERS (by James W. Fish)	27
V.	A NEVER-TO-BE-FORGOTTEN DAY	29
VI.	GOSPEL TENT WORK IN SOUTH AFRICA	34
VII.	OUR FIRST VISIT TO ROBBEN ISLAND	41
VIII.	EIGHT DAYS WITH THE LEPERS	44
IX.	THE LOVE OF CHRIST CONSTRAINETH	50
X.	GOSPEL WORK AMONG THE SOLDIERS DURING THE BOER WAR	75
XI.	A VISIT TO PONDOLAND	80
XII.	BACK TO ROBBEN ISLAND	86
XIII.	TROPHIES OF GRACE AMONG THE LEPERS	99
XIV.	"LONELY HEARTS TO CHERISH"	118
XV.	A TERRIBLE SCOURGE	138
XVI.	VISITS TO THE TRANSVAAL	157
XVII.	VISITORS TO THE ISLAND	160
XVIII.	"FAITH HEALERS" AT ROBBEN ISLAND	178
XIX.	"ONE SOWETH, ANOTHER REAPETH"	187
XX.	HOME AGAIN TO ENGLAND	206

FOREWORD

To reach mankind with "the Gospel of God" (Rom. i. 2), is a wonder of Almighty Grace. This is so, even when men and women are found in the ordinary circumstances of human life, in health, with minds able to receive the message and with hearts opened (Acts xvi. 14) to hear, and to welcome it unto salvation. This is surely no small mercy from God, for which we ought to be supremely thankful to Him for such Grace, in a world, over which the great Adversary has control, and exercises his authority and wiles, to hinder the spread of God's Good News among the sons of men. What a privilege to have liberty continued to declare the Word of Life, "publicly and from house to house" (Acts xx. 20)! And when "a great and effectual door" (1 Cor. xvi. 9), is manifestly opened to the servants of Christ, to enter with the message of His Grace, which He has been pleased to make the power of God unto salvation to all who believe (Rom. i. 16), in a sphere to which it is not generally possible to enter, this ought surely to draw forth the hearty, godly sympathies and fellowship of every Christian whose heart is in unison with the heart of God, in seeking the salvation of the perish-

FOREWORD

ing. Such a door has manifestly been opened and kept open for these thirty and odd years, among the lepers on Robben Island, for the Gospel, as made known to them by our esteemed friend and brother in the Lord, James W. Fish, his brother, Joseph, their helpers, and fellow-workers, with those visitors whom they have conducted thither, to the vast numbers of lepers who have been sent to that lone Isle, severed from the mass of mankind, to live and to die there, far from home and friends. To be " put in trust with the Gospel " (1 Thess. ii. 4), in any measure and in any sphere, is at all times a high honour as it is a great responsibility, but to have a door opened so manifestly of the Lord, as has been for these many years on Robben Island, for His servants who have so diligently carried the heaven-sent message of a present, full and free salvation through Jesus Christ the Lord, to a dying race, such as those lepers on this lone Isle are, is surely a ministry unique and unequalled in character, so far as we know, in any part of the great Mission Field. The dangers, to human life and limb, in the exercise of it are, as it seems to us, unprecedented. Journeys by sea and land, week by week, to the lone storm-beat Isle, to say nothing of discomforts and hardships, and the harrowing and ghastly sights which have to be witnessed among the leper patients suffering in all the stages of this dire disease, with the imminent dangers —as men reckon—of contagion from contact with the sufferers, is of itself enough to cause the stoutest heart to quell. Nothing less than the love of Christ indwelling and constraining the heart of any servant of the Lord, can lead him to go forth on and sustain

FOREWORD

him in such a service for the Lord's Name, as our esteemed friend and his fellow-helpers, have continued throughout these thirty-five odd years. They have not been in this service as the agents or servants of men, of any organization, or Society. They have simply been the free servants of the living God, looking direct to Him for His daily guidance in their service, depending upon Himself for all supplies, both spiritual and temporal, for the continuance of the work and counting on His faithfulness to provide "all things needful" for its fulfilment in a way worthy of Himself, and of the work that He has entrusted to them. And they bear their testimony to the fact, that He has *not failed* them in this, nor allowed themselves, their households, or the work they have sought to continue in His Name throughout the years, to lack anything needful for it. And all this, without either asking for, or receiving from the world or any of its resources of supply, a single shilling. This is indeed the Scriptural and old-fashioned way of carrying on " the work of the Lord " (1 Cor. xv. 58). And although it is neither popular, nor generally practised in our time, to serve the Lord in this way, it is, we believe, according to the pattern set forth in the Word of God, and after the example set by the first servants of the Lord, who went forth " everywhere preaching the Word" (Acts xi. 19). And here on Robben Island, as in the early years of the preaching of the Gospel, " the hand of the Lord has been with them, and a great number have believed and turned unto the Lord " (Acts xi. 21).

The *Diary* of the visitations and evangelisings of the

FOREWORD

lepers on Robben Island given in the following pages is a simple and unvarnished "Narrative of Facts," recorded, as they occurred from week to week. There has been no attempt made to elaborate them, to produce effect, or to magnify the workers or the work. The object of the narrative will have been attained, if it draws forth true, believing prayer for the lepers on Robben Island, from the Lord's Remembrancers in all lands, and supplication for the return (in the good will of God), of the Lord's servant, Mr James W. Fish, who is at present on a visit to this country—in renewed health and strength, to continue—in the will of the Lord—the work that lies so near his heart on Robben Island; and to raise up helpers to share in it; and so continue it for His Name in a godly and Scriptural way. To use the words of George Muller, of Bristol, written eighty-two years ago, concerning the simple, Scriptural lines upon which he carried on his service for the Lord among Orphans, with "the primary object," as he says, "to show before the whole world, and the whole church, that *even in these last days*, the *Living God* is ready to *prove* Himself the living God, by being ever willing to help, succour, comfort and sustain in His service, those who trust in Him, so that they need not go away from Him to their fellow-men or to *the ways of the world*, seeing that He is both able and willing to supply His servants with all they can need, in His service, and thus prove that there is after all, *reality in the right way of the Lord.*"

Kilmarnock, 30*th July* 1924.   JOHN RITCHIE.

THE LEPER'S CLEANSING AND RETURN

A beautiful Poem, written many years ago, which I read as a lad, is so truthful and touching, that I give it a place in this Narrative of "Gospel Grace, among the Lepers of Robben Island. This very same Lord Jesus," though now enthroned in Heavenly Glory, is still working miracles of mercy, and spiritual healing, in the souls of men, and bringing them to His feet as disciples and worshippers.

THE LEPER'S CLEANSING AND RETURN.

"A man *full* of leprosy." (Luke v. 12).
"I will; be thou clean." (Mark i. 41).
"The lepers are cleansed." (Matt. xi. 5).

" ' Room for the leper! room ! ' and as he came
The cry passed on—' Room for the leper ! room ! '
Room for the leper ! and aside they stood,
Matron and child, and pitiless manhood—all
Who met him on his way—and let him pass,
And onward, through the open gate he came,
A leper, with the ashes on his brow,
Sackcloth about his loins, and on his lip
A covering : stepping painfully and slow,
And with a difficult utterance, like one
Whose heart is with an iron nerve put down—
Crying, ' Unclean ! unclean ! '

" 'Twas now the depth
Of the Judean summer, and the leaves,
Whose shadows lay so still upon the path,
That budded on the clear and flashing eye
Of Judah's loftiest noble. He was young
And eminently beautiful, and life
Mantled in eloquent fulness on his lip,
And sparkled in his glance ; and in his mien
There was a gracious pride, that every eye
Followed with benisons—and this was he.

THE LEPER'S CLEANSING AND RETURN

With the soft air of summer there had come
A torpor on his frame, which not the speed
Of his best barb, nor music, nor the blast
Of the bold huntsmen's horn, nor aught that stirs
The spirit of its bent, might drive away :
The blood beat not as wont within his veins ;
Dimness crept o'er his eye : A drowsy sloth
Fettered his limbs like palsy, and his past
With all its loftiness, seemed struck with eld,
Even his voice was changed—a languid moan
Taking the place of the clear silver key ;
And brain and sense grew faint, as if the light
And very air were steeped in sluggishness.
He strove with it awhile, as manhood will,
Ever too proud for weakness, till the rein
Slackened within his grasp, and in its poise
The arrowy jereed like an aspen shook :
Day after day, he lay as if in sleep ;
His skin grew dry and bloodless, and white scales
Circled with livid purple, covered him.
And then his nails grew black, and fell away
From the dull flesh about them, and the hues
Deepened beneath the hard unmoistened scales
And from their edges grew the rank white hair,
—And Helon *was a leper !*

" Day was breaking
Where at the altar of the Temple, stood
The holy priest of God. The incense lamp
Burned with a struggling light, and a low chant
Swelled thro' the hollow arches of the roof
Like an articulate wail, and there alone,
Wasted to ghastly thinness, Helon knelt.
The echoes of the melancholy strain
Died in the distant aisles : and he rose up,
Struggling with weakness, and bowed his head
Upon the sprinkled ashes, and put off
His costly raiment, for the leper's garb :
And with the sackcloth round him, and his lip

THE LEPER'S CLEANSING AND RETURN

Hid in loathsome covering, stood still,
Waiting to hear his *doom:*—

"'Depart! depart! O child
Of Israel, from the Temple of thy God;
For He has smote thee with the chastening rod.
And to the desert wild,
From all thou lovest, away thy feet must flee
That from thy plague, His people may be free:

"'Depart, and come not near
The busy mart, the crowded city more,
Nor set thy foot a human threshold o'er;
And stay thou not to hear
Voices that call thee in the way: and fly
From all who in the wilderness pass by.

"'Wet not thy burning lip
In streams that to a human dwelling glide,
Nor rest thee where the covert fountains hide:
Nor kneel thee down to drink,
By desert-well, or river's grassy brink.

"'And pass not thou between
The weary traveller and the cooling breeze;
And lie not down to sleep beneath the trees
Where *human* tracks are seen:
Nor milk the goat that browseth on the plains,
Nor pluck the standing corn, or yellow grain.

"'And now depart! and when
Thy heart is heavy and thine eyes are dim,
Lift up thy prayer beseechingly to Him
Who, from the tribes of man,
Selected thee, to feel His chastening rod.
Depart, O leper! and forget not God!'
And he went forth—*alone*; not one of all
The many whom he loved. Nor she whose name
Was woven in the fibres of his heart,

THE LEPER'S CLEANSING AND RETURN

Breaking within her now, to come and speak
Comfort to him. Yes, he went his way,
Sick and heart-broken and alone, to die ;
For God had cursed the leper !

"It was noon,
And Helon knelt beside a stagnant pool
In the lone wilderness, and bathed his brow,
Hot with the burning leprosy—and touched
The loathsome water to his parched lips,
Praying that he might be so blessed—*to die* !

" Footsteps approached, and with no strength to flee
He drew the covering closer to his lip—
Crying, ' Unclean ! unclean ! ' and in the folds
Of the coarse sackcloth shrouding up his face
He fell upon the earth till they should pass.

" Nearer the Stranger came, and bending o'er
The leper's prostrate form, pronounced his name,
' HELON ! '—the voice was like the master tone
Of a rich instrument—most strangely sweet ;
And the dull pulses of disease awoke.
And for a moment beat beneath the hot
And leprous scales with a restoring thrill—
' Helon, arise ! ' and he forgot his curse
And arose and stood before Him.

"Love and awe,
Mingled in the regard of Helon's eye
As he beheld the Stranger. He was not
In costly raiment clad, nor on his brow
The symbol of a Princely lineage wore :
No followers at His back, nor in His hand
Buckler, or sword, or spear :—Yet in His mien
Command sat throned serene ; and if He smiled,
A kindly condescension graced His lips—
The lion would have crouched to Him, within his lair ;

THE LEPER'S CLEANSING AND RETURN

His garb was simple and His sandals worn,
His statue modelled with a perfect grace,
His countenance the impress of a god,
Touched with the open innocence of a child ;
His eye was blue and calm, as is the sky
In the serenest noon ; His hair unshorn
Fell on His shoulders, and His curling beard
The fulness of perfected manhood bore :
He looked on Helon earnestly awhile
As if His heart was moved : and stooping down
He took a little water in His hands,
He laid it on his brow and said ' Be clean ! '
And lo ! the scales fell from him, and his blood
Coursed with delicious coolness thro' his veins,
And his dry palms grew moist, and on his brow
The dewy softness of an infant stole.
His leprosy was cleansed, and he fell down
Prostrate at JESUS' feet, and worshipped Him."

CHAPTER II.

THE EARLY HISTORY OF ROBBEN ISLAND.

PROBABLY but few of the residents on the sea coast of Cape Colony, give more than an occasional passing thought to the little barren-looking patch of land, situated at the mouth of Table Bay, known as Robben Island, or the Isle of Seals. It is, however, an object of much interest to those who arrive for the first time in South Africa by the mail steamers. For who can be unmoved on first hearing of the inhabitants who are inmates of its various institutions—the Law-breakers, the Lunatics, and the Lepers!

Few places probably, so small and insignificant-looking, can boast of having played so important a part in the history of a vast multitude of people, as can this little island in the rise, progress, and present welfare of the Cape Colony. I make no apology, therefore, in calling the attention of the readers of my narrative to the Island's early history. And I claim for it more than a momentary passing attention. I ask for a respectful and reverential regard. And I assert that it has a right to such, for the pages of South African history tell of strange events here in the far-off past, and the existence of ancient ruins on the island, recently brought to light, speak of

THE EARLY HISTORY OF ROBBEN ISLAND

busy scenes, and many hands at work, in days long gone by. We first hear of the Island in the year 1591, in connection with the visit of an Englishman, a sea-captain, by name Raymond, who sailed from Plymouth for the East Indies, on the 10th April, in command of three English vessels, *The Penelope, The Merchant Royal,* and *The Edward Bonaventure.* He found the place uninhabited, but seals and penguin's were seen in large numbers. This visit of Raymond, took place just ninety years after the arrival of Antonio de Salanha, the Portuguese captain, who was the first European known to have landed in Table Bay, to have ascended Table Mountain for reconnoitring purposes, and to have established the Cape as a place for watering ships.

We do not know that Joao de Nova, who set sail from Portugal in 1501, and discovered the Island of Ascension on his outward voyage, and on his return journey from Mossel Bay, passed the Cape, and discovered the Island of St Helena, who stepping ashore there, added it to his island discoveries. Nor have we the honour of giving the story of Bartholomew Diaz, who in 1486 claimed South Africa for Christ, as he reared the Cross on a little island in Algoa Bay; nor of Vasco de Gama, the explorer of still greater fame. No! the name of our discoverer is unknown, unless it be the worthy Englishman, Captain Raymond himself, who in 1591 found seals and penguins in such plenty.

There is, however, a rumour abroad, that previous to this, the Portuguese had tried to establish some kind of settlement on the island, but had failed in the attempt. Possibly the true facts may ere long be unearthed, from the archives of Lisbon.

The next recorded visit of a European to the island, is that of one Joris van Spilbergen, who sailed for the East Indies from Vere in Zeeland, in command of three vessels, *The Ram*, *The Schaap*, and *The Lam*. He landed on 2nd December 1601, and gave to the island the name of Cornelia. He, too, was struck with the vast number of seals and penguins which he saw.

It appears that in these early years, European voyages and settlers at the Cape, found much difficulty at times in providing themselves with sufficient food ; owing to incivility or unwillingness on the part of, or actual warfare with, the native tribes living in the neighbourhood of Table Bay, it was impossible to procure any supplies. And so we find that Robben Island proved to be to the first Colonists a veritable " Treasure Island," it being their only source of constant food supply.

It is recorded that meat being scarce, they sent off a vessel to Coney (Dassen) Island for penguins and conies, which they " salted in," and on their return they left two conies on Cornelia Island, and shot seven or eight sheep (left by previous voyagers), and took their carcases on board.

A few years later, in 1608, we hear of a Dutch Admiral, Cornelius Maaklof, leaving rams and ewes here, and in the following year a certain Captain Keelay took off the island some of the " fattest sheep he ever saw," and left lean ones in exchange.

But not only did the Island afford a welcome supply of fresh mutton to the mariners of those days,

THE EARLY HISTORY OF ROBBEN ISLAND

it also proved to be a mine of wealth to the merchant trader. Captain Nicholas Dounton, of the East India Company, homeward bound, saw "two Dutch ships at anchor in Table Bay, laden with oil which had been collected from Robben Island." This was in July 1610, and in the year 1611, Isaac le Marie, a skipper, left his son Jacob, and a party of seamen, in order to kill seals on the island, and to harpoon whales. We are not told what great fortunes were realised by these early dwellers on these shores, but on one occasion no fewer than 4005 seal-skins were sent to the European market. At times, too, the flesh of the seals was salted to provide for seasons of scarcity, which were not uncommon.

Sir Thomas Herbert, in his *Travels*, says that it was considered advisable to found a Fort at the Cape of Good Hope, for the insurance of the refreshment so necessary to navigators, and for the preservation of the seafaring people. So much was this felt to be needed, that at the special request of the English East India Company, a party of ten Englishmen, who had been sentenced at the Old Bailey, London, to punishment for crime, was sent out in 1614 under Captain Payton, with a view to establish a settlement on Robben Island. It was thought that they could keep up a supply of fresh provisions for passing ships.

This venture, however, proved no more successful than the supposed previous Portuguese attempt. For quarrels with the natives on the mainland ensued, and the leader of the party, Cross by name, was killed. Four of his men were drowned in trying to board an English vessel, and only three succeeded in escaping home. Whether or no the remaining two ended their days here, is not recorded, but possibly they were found living in Robinson Crusoe style by the two Englishmen, Captains Shillinge and Fitzherbert, who, in 1620, claimed the Cape of Good Hope for England, under King James the First.

It appears that England did not see fit to make good this claim. And for a considerable number of years, little or nothing is known of the history of these parts. At length, in 1648, the silence is broken by the report of some shipwrecked Dutch sailors of the vessel *Haarlem*, who, having spent five months ashore in Table Bay, strongly recommended the establishment of a Fort and a Garrison at the Cape, by the Dutch East India Company. In response to this appeal, Holland sent out her first expedition under Jan Antony van Riebeck, in command of three vessels, the *Dromedary*, the *Heron*, and the *Goede Hoop*. They set sail on 14th December 1651, and arrived in sight of Robben Island on 5th April 1652.

So great was the interest of those first Dutch Colonists, in this little Isle, that, shortly after his arrival at the Cape, van Riebeck insisted on landing on the island in person. It is told how at this time, Table Bay was full of whales, and a council was held how best to profit by them; how in crossing over to the island the Commander nearly lost his life, and how, on landing, he and his shooting party bagged a hundred sea-birds, and took three thousand eggs. It was seen at a glance, how exceedingly good the pasturage was, and how valuable a possession the island would at once become to them. Such, for a time, it proved to

THE EARLY HISTORY OF ROBBEN ISLAND

be, for it produced shells (both land and sea varieties), which were burnt for lime; slate of the best quality for building purposes; fine fat sheep and rabbits in abundance, birds with their eggs innumerable, and chief of all, seals and whales in very large quantities.

In 1654, we read, a small party of men was stationed on the island to collect seal-skins and oil, and to look after the sheep. Again, in 1655, 300 sheep were purchased from Gounema, a native tribe of Saldanha Bay, and placed on the island as a reserve stock, the pasturage being still good. "About 500 ewes were then kept on the island by the Company, for breeding purposes. But a few years later, a virulent sickness carried off all but 35 of the 500, and it was noticed in 1662 that a species of snake, harmless to man,—had of late so greatly increased, that the rabbits could not multiply further. So they stocked some of the islands in Saldanha Bay with rabbits, as a food supply in case of scarcity.

Still, in spite of these difficulties, Robben Island grew rapidly in value and in importance.

In 1657, (a year of much activity in the Public Works and Native Affairs Department), " a platform was erected on the highest point on the island, upon which a fire was kept burning at nights whenever ships of the Company were seen off the port," and a treaty with the natives was drawn up by Van Riebeck dealing kindly with them, but stating that if any of them assaulted or robbed a burgher, those suspected would be seized and placed on Robben Island, and, if found guilty, would be kept there as prisoners, for two or more years.

ROBBEN ISLAND

The first of a long succession of prisoners whose names find a place in the island's history, was one Harry (or Herry), a leading native trader and interpreter between the Dutch and his own people. He, together with two companions in misfortune, Khamy (or van Kou), and Simon Boubo by name, were placed here for safety and to be out of mischief, rather than for punishment. But the wily Harry made good his escape in an old leaky boat, to Saldanha Bay.

Shortly after this, on the 9th June 1665, news of an outbreak of a much more serious nature, reached the authorities. War had broken out between the English and the Dutch. Naturally, it was at once asked, " Is our Fort strong enough to withstand such an attack ? " " No ! " was the decided reply. " We must build a strong fortress with guns and garrison." Forthwith, 300 men were employed, and a certain Peter Dombaar, an engineer, with a party of convicts and slaves was sent to Robben Island to gather shells, and three or four large-decked boats were constantly to be seen transporting the shells (as well as fuel from Hout Bay) for the lime kilns. Thus was begun the famous " Castle " of Capetown, the four foundation stones of which were laid on 2nd June 1666. Not only did the island supply the lime for this historic building, but also much of the dressed stone used in its construction.

So important did the work on the island become, that it required the presence of a resident overseer; whereupon one Pieter van Meerhof was appointed. This man was by birth a Dane, who had come to Africa as a soldier, and as he had some knowledge

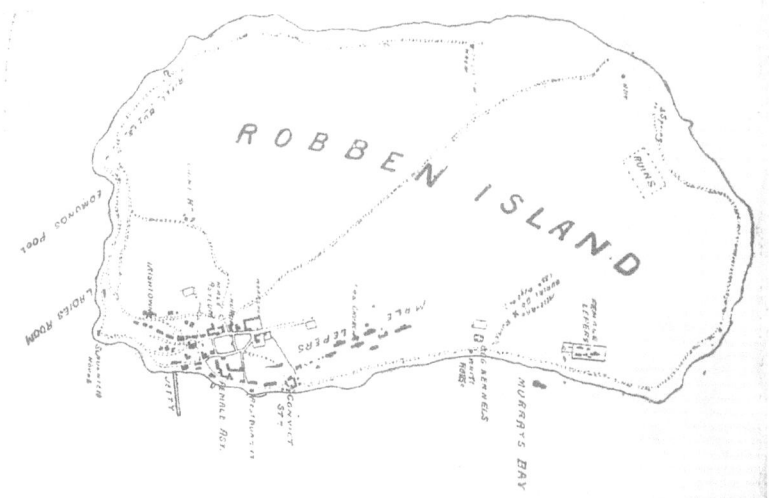

Plan of Robben Island.

Landing at the Island in early days.

Motor boat leaving the island for the steamboat with unusually calm sea.

of dressing wounds, he was chosen as under-surgeon of the Company. On the strength of this appointment, and doubtless not liking to face alone the isolation and solitariness of the island life, he bravely took to himself a wife in the person of one Eva, who had been acting as interpreter for the Dutch (perhaps in Harry's absence), and who is believed to have been the first Christian Hottentot in South Africa.

If this be so (and there is little reason to doubt it), Robben Island can perhaps boast of having been the home of the first Christian native, south of the Equator; for Eva accompanied her husband to the island, and lived here with him for about three years. Once, she crossed over to the mainland, for the christening of a child. In 1667, she had a fall and injured herself severely, and in the same year, sad to relate, her husband, who had been sent as head of an expedition to the Mauritius and Madagascar, met with death at the hands of some natives. The widow, Eva, survived her husband for seven years, part of which she spent on the island, and part on the mainland, living a careless and somewhat disreputable life. She was, nevertheless, buried in the Church at the Castle, as having been the first baptized Hottentot.

A year after van Meerhof's death, we hear of an island prisoner of some note, by name Henry Lawes, who, having embezzled stores, was reduced to the rank of a common soldier, and subsequently sent to Batavia; also of a Malay political prisoner in irons, one of three criminals brought from Batavia. It is of some interest to note the crimes of which the offenders were found guilty in those days, and the style of punishment they

ROBBEN ISLAND

had to undergo, but, this is not altogether pleasant reading, so a few specimen cases will suffice. In 1670, a Dutchman named Willems was banished to the island for accidentally shooting a native. In 1671, five Hottentot Cochoqua prisoners were sent over, having been first flogged and branded, for sheep stealing and assault. Three of them were sentenced to fifteen years, and the other two to seven years. But they all made their escape in a boat. In 1672, Thuintje van Warden, wife of a burgher, having been found guilty of evil speaking against other women, " was sentenced to retract the slander, ask forgiveness, be bound to a post for one hour, and then suffer banishment for six weeks on Robben Island. Soon after this, two soldiers were flogged and sent to work in irons for four months, for stealing a few vegetables, " an offence tending to the ruin of this growing Colony." On the 17th August of the same year, J. Jans, a freeman, being found guilty of picking the pockets of a drunken man, had his property confiscated, was flogged, and sent to work in chains for three years. It is recorded of him that he also intoxicated his dogs and pigs by giving them sugar and eggs, mixed with wine. His punishment was slight, compared with that of two mutinous soldiers who were flogged and sentenced to twenty-five years' hard labour in chains. In 1673, Tryntje Theunissen, N. Cornelissen, and Jan Theunissen, for stealing two cows and slaughtering them, were bound to posts with a cowhide over their heads, flogged, branded, and sent to Robben Island for twelve years, besides having to make good the stolen cattle, and forfeit all their

THE EARLY HISTORY OF ROBBEN ISLAND

property. In 1675, two slaves, for a theft of vegetables, had their ears cut off and were kept in chains on Robben Island for life. Enough of such horrors!

During this time, war was being carried on between France and England on the one side, under Louis XIV. and Charles II., and the United Provinces on the other, and preparations were made on the island to abandon the works if an enemy appeared, and to destroy all the " plant," that could not be carried off. But no such luck! For more than a hundred years, no enemy came in sight, and so in all probability, during these many years, the island continued to be the scene of much cruelty and tyranny.

> " Truly, this Island could a tale unfold,
> Of many a dark deed, done in days of old."

And it is said, that

> " Many a treasure lies beneath its sands
> Hid in those early years, by shipwrecked hands,"

For on 20th January 1694, the yacht *Dageraad*(?) laden with cargo and specie, from Goude Bay, ran ashore and became a wreck, on the rock-bound western side of the island, and sixteen of her crew were drowned. This is but one instance of many shipping disasters that have taken place, on these rugged shores.

From 1694 to 1764, little or anything seems to be known of the island's history. Here and there only, we get a brief glimpse of what was going on.

It appears that the staff of labourers was much reduced, the Castle having then been completed: yet

ROBBEN ISLAND

the quarrying of slate continued. Many of the best of the old-fashioned Cape Town stoeps, and some of the finest tombstones in the cemeteries still bear witness to the good quality of the output from the Robben Island quarries. The flat stones used for the stoep of the old Burgher Watch House (the present Cape " Town House "), the foundation stone of which was laid on 18th November 1755, in Governor Rijk Tulbagh's time, were obtained from the island. Most of these stones are 14 inches square, and it is stated that the sum of 90 Rix dollars was paid for 700 stones. (A Rix dollar was worth 1s. 6d.)

All through this period, too, the island continued to be used as a place of banishment for prisoners, and from these days up to the present, this has been one of its special features. Amongst them one man of note must not be left unmentioned, namely, the King of Madura, in the Presidency of Madras, who in 1772, was transported from his dominions, by order of the Dutch East India Company.

Two other notable persons paid a visit to the island about this time, within a few years of each other. During the Governorship of Rijk Tulbagh, in 1764, Lord Clive visited the Cape on his way to India for the last time. During his stay, he was driven by a South-easter in one of the ship's boats to the island, and he and his crew spent the night ashore. In October 1776, Captain Cook, of " Round the World " celebrity, took away with him a number of rabbits, with a view to stocking New Zealand, Otahwite, and other places.

The French traveller and naturalist, Le Voillant,

THE EARLY HISTORY OF ROBBEN ISLAND

says, writing of this period : " The island takes its name from the number of marine dogs that are found there ; it is under the charge of a corporal who has the title of " Commander." Its unhappy exiles had each day to deliver a certain quantity of limestone, which they dug. In spare time they fished, or cultivated their small gardens, which procured them tobacco, as well as some other little indulgences."

This brings us to the close of the last century. It has been the purpose of the writer of this brief sketch to deal only with the island's early history, leaving to some future occasion, perhaps, the continuance of the story up to the present time. It will be a satisfaction to him, if by putting together the foregoing historical facts, and presenting them to the public in an easily readable form, he has succeeded in proving that Robben Island has always been a valuable possession to its owners.

If our predecessors, the Dutch, found it to be so, much more do we English, its present owners, set store by it. And though we cannot speak of it as

> " The best and brighest gem,
> In Britain's southern diadem,"

still it has its undoubted value, and it is no exaggeration to say, that it continues to play no small part, in the welfare and progress of Cape Colony.

G. F. GRESLEY.

CHAPTER III.
THE HISTORY OF LEPROSY.

EGYPT was regarded by the Ancients (positively by Lucretius) as the country from whence Leprosy came. " Pline implies that it was introduced by the army of Pompey returning from Syria." At St Gall in the 8th, and at Canterbury in the 11th Century, leprosy grew to be epidemic in Western Europe. It attacked the people in great numbers, and in all ranks (including members of royal families). Leper houses (mostly religious, and dedicated to St Lazarus) were raised. In Northern Europe they were more secular, and dedicated to St George. These were founded in every considerable town in Britain.

The total number of such in Europe, was loosely estimated by Matthew Paris at 19,000. The number in France is independently estimated at 2000, and (according to Sir J. Y. Simpson) there were 95 houses of the first class in England, (of these 7 at Norwich, and 5 at Linn), with several in Ireland and in Scotland. The isolation of lepers was strictly enforced by law, and by popular sentiment. They wore a special costume, usually a long grey gown, with hood drawn over the face, and each carried a wooden clapper to give warning of their approach. They were forbidden to enter inns, churches, mills or bakehouses, to touch healthy persons, or to eat with them, to wash in the streams, or to walk in narrow footpaths. Their outcast state

THE HISTORY OF LEPROSY

was signified by the German name (*Aussots*). The Chronicle of Limburg (under the year 1374), speaks of a famous monkish poet, whose songs all Germany was singing, as one " Derward von din Lenten Aussatzig, und war nicht rein."

The disease began to decline (first in Italy) in the 15th Century, and had mostly disappeared in the 17th.

A leper house was founded in Edinburgh (in Greenside) as late as 1591, and it was not till 1741 (others give 1798) that the last known leper, died in Shetland.

The disease diverges into two main varieties. The spotted (leper macu-losa), and the nodular (leper tuberculosa). The two kinds are found side by side in the same population, and sometimes in the same person.

Leprosy has been claimed as one of the diseases caused by parasites, on several occasions by old writers of long ago, and recently by observers who have found innumerable minute bacillus-rods within the cells of the leprous new growth. The essential cause of leprosy is unknown. It probably arose in the Delta and Valley of the Nile, in prehistoric times, and under similar climatic and telluric conditions in other (chiefly interpical) countries. One of the most memorable facts in its history is, its rise and subsidence, as an epidemic disease in Europe.

It is now endemic (chiefly, but not exclusively) among those who inhabit the sea coast, or the estuaries of rivers, who live much on fish (often putrid), and who intermarry closely.

ROBBEN ISLAND

Dr Black says : "Leprosy, in my experience, is far too apt to be considered as an affliction of the integument mucous members, and peripheral nerves, with various secondary changes in the bones, etc. From evidence which I shall produce, however, I believe when leprosy deposit begins to take place in the integument, it also forms in the *liver* and *spleen*.

"Neither in the heart, nor lungs, nor in their searious members, have I ever found any evidence of leprotic infiltration.

"The leprosy bacilli have been found in the discharge from the bowel, and it must be remembered that this may be a main source of spread of the bacilli. On a microscopic examination of the liver and spleen, I found the typical cell infiltration, the cells being full of bacilli. I consider this an important observation, for it seems to show that in maculo-anaesthetic leprosy, even when after a lapse of time, the morbid process in the skin and nerves has died out, there may still be insusceptible internal, and active leprous deposit, and that the patient may still be a source of infection through alvine discharge.

"From my observations I conclude that a large part of the life history of the bacillus take place in the interior of these cells, and that cellular proliferation is necessary for its development. Of course, the containing cell is frequently broken up, and spores in the bacilli are thus scattered, for further development. They, therefore, need to be taken up by other similar cells.

"It is on this account that I have stated above, that I attach no special importance to the presence of scattered or stray bacilli not contained in cells, in various parts of the body. For when the cells which contain the bacilli break up, these micro-organisms are bound to be carried away by the blood stream, and deposited as mere debris when the current slackens."

The point which struck me most, is the absence of degeneration of cells, and of caseation caused by the bacilli.

A few tubercle bacilli cause caseation of the surrounding cells by their excreted toxin, whereas multitudes of leper bacilli only, cause such an effect by the pressure of their accumulation.

It is this malign benignity, which makes the disease so hopeless.

As will be noted throughout in the following pages of the *Diary* of visitations among the lepers on Robben Island, during recent years much has been done giving partial relief to leprous patients, and many mitigations to the disease in its various forms have been discovered, practised and applied by medical science and experience. But so far as is at present known, no permanent *cure* for this awful malady has yet been found. Like inbred sin in the soul of man, of which leprosy is the type—it needs the Divine Hand to affect a true discharge from this awful disease and all its effects.

Another witness to the "Nature and Progress of Leprosy," which appeared in *The British Herald* many years ago, is well worth recording here. "The disease of Leprosy is said to begin *within* the body—in the marrow bones and blood. A sanious moisture

ROBBEN ISLAND

is thrown out. Then it makes its appearance in small spots on the skin. "These increase in size and in number and at last completely cover the whole body, making the poor leper a terrible spectacle." Another says: "The disease advances from one stage to another, with slow and certain ruin. Life lingers around the desolation. The joints and hands and the feet lose their power, and the whole body collapses or falls together in a form awful and hideous. In one form of the disease in which it commences in the extremities, the joints separate, the fingers, toes and other members fall off one by one, and the malady thus gradually approaches the seat of life. The victim is thus doomed to see himself dying piecemeal, assured that no human power can arrest the steady march of the dire disease to the seat of life." It is contagious and hereditary, and is often transmitted to the third or fourth generations.

CHAPTER IV.

THIRTY-FOUR YEARS AMONGST THE LEPERS.

DIARY OF JAMES W. FISH.

THE following extracts from my diary are sent forth with one desire : that GOD may be glorified. It is through the Grace of the Lord JESUS, that we have been enabled to continue, " lo these many years," telling forth the story of the love of GOD the FATHER, as manifested in JESUS CHRIST THE LORD, as set forth under the direction of the Holy Spirit in the Book of Books, the Bible, which has proved so comforting to very many of the poor, afflicted lepers.

Should the perusal of this narrative bring some of God's children to their knees before the throne of Grace on behalf of the patients of the Leper Institute on Robben Island, the writer will be well repaid.

These poor sufferers need your prayers, the Hospital staff needs them : those who seek to win their souls for God and to cheer their dark days with His Word, need them. Will you meet that need, or shall the work languish because you are too busy to pray ? " The heartfelt supplication of a righteous man, exerts a mighty influence," (James, v. 16, Weymouth).

Because I found it interesting and instructive, I have inserted in this narrative a portion of *The Early*

ROBBEN ISLAND

History of Robben Island, compiled by G. F. Gresley, with whom I have been acquainted for many years. And it is with his full consent that it is inserted herein. It will be seen that the island has been full of interest all the years ever since it was first discovered.

Mr J. F. Goch, " my fellow-labourer in the Gospel," continues his fellowship with me in the work by writing an introduction also. I take this opportunity of thanking him for so doing, and praise God for the happy fellowship we have had together in proclaiming " liberty to the captives," and " the opening of the prison to them that are bound."

Mr JOHN RITCHIE, the Publisher, has written a FOREWORD to the narrative, setting forth in few words the Scriptural principles on which the work has been carried on throughout the years, which may God richly bless, in stirring up godly, prayerful fellowship in the continuance of it on the same lines as set forth in His Word.

To all those who have accompanied either my brother or myself to the Island, my thanks is warmly tendered, and my earnest request to them is " DON'T STOP PRAYING."

CHAPTER V.
DEPARTURE FOR SOUTH AFRICA.

A NEVER-TO-BE-FORGOTTEN DAY.

29th *February* 1889, is a never-to-be-forgotten day in our life's history.

On that dark English winter morning, with the stars brightly shining, under the glorious canopy of heaven, and long before the sun had made his appearance, my brother Joseph and I, with our large Gospel Tent, on board the s.s. *Delhi*, moved out of the Cardiff Docks, bound for Port Elizabeth, South Africa.

Our hearts were naturally sore, as we had just bidden farewell to our dear, aged, widowed mother. And for anything we knew, probably not to meet her again in this life.

We had heard the call distinctly " Come over and help us " (Acts xvi. 9), and we felt that we must obey it, at all costs.

It was very touching to us, as the boat moved slowly through the docks, to see in the glimmer of the lamps, a few dear warm-hearted fellow-saints, who, in spite of the cold, in the early hours of that morning, had come to show the sincerity of their love.

Amongst the number, was a beloved sister, Mrs Matthews, a dear, godly saint; our faithful fellow-labourer, Mr George Maskell; and one or two members of our own family besides.

ROBBEN ISLAND

We were soon lost to the sight of each other, but only to the natural eye, thank God. For with the Christian it is not " out of sight out of mind " ; at least it surely ought not so to be.

We had then time to settle down to the great task which lay before us.

The following lines were written, and handed to the pilot on his leaving the boat :—

Parting Verses composed off Penarth Head (Rev. xxi. 1-4).

> To those we love so dearly
> We bid a long farewell ;
> To foreign shores we journey,
> The Saviour's love to tell.
>
> How dear each one is to us,
> As friend from friend now part !
> And as they say " God bless you,"
> Their love doth touch our heart.
>
> But whilst we think of partings,
> Which oft must us give pain,
> We have that precious promise,
> We all shall see again.
>
> And oh ! that blissful union,—
> When never more we part ;
> When Christ shall be the glory,
> And He shall fill our heart.
>   J. and J. FISH, s.s. *Delhi*.

The first part of our voyage was rather eventful. The pilot had not left us very long, before the wind from the west increased in strength, and the boat began to pitch heavily, at times dipping her bows clean under the sea, the violence of the waves becoming worse during the night.

A NEVER-TO-BE-FORGOTTEN DAY

About nine o'clock the following morning, the second officer, with two or three men, was on the forecastle, and while in the act of furling a sail, a heavy sea struck the boat, carrying overboard the second officer and one of the sailors. The latter was washed on board again, but the " second " was drowned, in spite of every effort to save him. This cast a gloom over all on board, no one feeling it more than Captain Thompson. My brother and I, however, had reason to believe that the second officer was a Christian. Hence the few lines written the following day.

Lines written on the death of the Second Mate of the s.s. Delhi, *who was drowned off Land's End on the outward-bound voyage of the two brothers James and Joseph Fish for S. Africa.*

> Where is the one we saw so bright
> At table on that morn ?
> And thought we saw a heavenly light,
> Upon his features dawn ?
>
> There was something in his manner
> That spake of peace within ;
> That he possessed that precious gift
> The Christ, Who saves from sin.
>
> Where is he now ? we ask again ?
> He found a watery grave ;
> The storm had hurled him overboard ;
> Himself he could not save.
>
> But where is he that lived within
> That mortal form of clay ?
> Is he beneath the cruel waves,
> For ever there to stay ?
>
> Ah ! no, his soul has gone above ;
> From sin and death set free ;
> To see the One he loved so well,
> And in His presence be.

ROBBEN ISLAND

> And Oh ! the joy of that blest place,
> From sorrow free and pain ;
> Of such an one we can but say,
> " For him to die, is gain."
>
> JAS. and JOS. FISH.

Our voyage henceforth was fairly pleasant, and we had the privilege of holding a Service on board whenever we wished. We are quite confident that the Captain himself was brought to the Lord, during our voyage to the Cape.

The 26th of March, found us safely anchored in Algoa Bay.

We went ashore with the Captain the following day, and got our first letters. And Oh ! the unspeakable joy that filled our hearts, when we read of the conversion of our own dear mother !

It perhaps would not be out of place to insert just here, a letter from a sister, giving her account of that event.

CAMBRIDGE STREET,
February 29th.

MY DEAR BROTHER IN THE LORD,

Just one line of greeting on your arrival, and to say that we have been continually " wishing you God-speed " ever since you left us, which seems more like three months than less than three weeks.

I thought that you would like to know that I have been in twice to see your dear mother, who received me very kindly.

We talked freely of you, which led to the

A NEVER-TO-BE-FORGOTTEN DAY

theme of God's great love to us, and I felt confident she was anxious. And we know how your hearts will rejoice, when you get the good news that she has at last confessed to trusting in our Lord Jesus Christ, as her Saviour. The Lord keep her.

I am so sorry that I have not been able to see her since Tuesday, owing to weakness.

Now we are all longing much to hear from you.

Leaving you in His dear hands, grace, and love be with you.

   Believe me,

     Yours in Eternal Bonds,

  M. A. B.

CHAPTER VI.

GOSPEL TENT WORK IN SOUTH AFRICA.

My brother and I at once took steps with a view to the erection of our large Gospel Tent, and we hired a piece of ground for it in the heart of the city. But to our great surprise next day, just when arrangements were being made to land the tent, the Captain told us that his cargo had been sold to a Cape Town agent, for the Colonial Government, and that he was most anxious to get the boat away that same afternoon if possible.

" Could we change our plans, and come round with him ? "

This indeed was remarkable, for, as a matter of fact, Cape Town was the very place to which we had originally intended going, but could not find a boat sailing from Cardiff, to take us there.

However, after talking and praying over the matter, we decided to go round.

" By faith Abraham, when he was called to go out, obeyed, and he went out, not knowing whither he went " (Heb. xi. 8).

We left Algoa Bay on 28th March, at 6 p.m. The next morning the sun shone brightly, wind and tide were in our favour, reminding us of Paul's experience in Acts xxvii. 13, of " the south wind that

GOSPEL TENT WORK IN SOUTH AFRICA

blew softly," soon to be followed by " a tempestuous wind." Little did we know what was awaiting us, before another twenty-four hours.

We were busy all day packing up, and getting ready our tent, as we expected to arrive in Table Bay the next evening.

About five o'clock in the morning, we were startled by hearing two very heavy crashes; the second one nearly throwing us out of our berths.

For the moment we were a little excited, my own thought being that we had acted the part of Jonah, and had refused to erect our tent at *Nineveh*. But not so my brother. He declined to believe that that tent had been made, to go down to the bottom of the sea. How one learns in such experiences the truth of Eccles. iv. 9-10, and also the wisdom of our Lord in choosing and sending forth his witnesses " two and two " (Luke x. 1). However, our fears were soon allayed; it was discovered that the boat had struck a coral reef, and being an old P. and O. mail boat, strongly built, she broke herself away, without much damage. Through the mercy of our ever-gracious God, we arrived safely in Table Bay on Saturday evening, 30th of March.

We landed our tent on Monday, and after prayer and consultation with brethren at Wynberg, we decided to make a commencement there. The following Wednesday we held our first Tent Service, continuing each evening for six weeks. The people came out well, the tent being too small on Sunday evenings. We had the joy of leading many souls to Christ, also of baptizing and receiving them into Christian fellowship.

ROBBEN ISLAND

Our next move was two miles off, in a place along the line to Claremont. Here our faith was to be very much tested. We were not altogether satisfied with the position of our tent, and soon found that our apprehensions were not without some foundation. We had hired a front room, from which we could see the tent, from the house of a Veterinary Surgeon, a " Seventh Day Adventist." One evening at the close of the Service, feeling much cast upon God, we sought Him earnestly for a *sure token* of His mind regarding the position of the tent, something we could not fail to understand. We learned afterwards that the Surgeon who was present, was deeply impressed by the definite petition. " If a son shall ask bread of any of you that is a father, will he give give him a stone ? " (Luke xi. 11).

That same night, just before my brother and I retired to rest, I drew the blind aside and peered through the window toward the tent, only to find it reeling to and fro with the wind. At once we dressed, crept out quietly, took it down, or it blew down (one must have the experience to understand what this means in a south-east gale). And by two or three o'clock in the morning, we had it snugly packed away against a corrugated-iron fence which covered it from the view of the house. At six o'clock, just as the Surgeon left the house on his usual rounds, his eyes fell upon the spot where, only the night before, he had listened to that definite request, and to his great surprise, which almost shocked him, no tent was to be seen. He told us afterwards, that for a moment,

GOSPEL TENT WORK IN SOUTH AFRICA

he really thought that the tent had been carried up into the clouds. I mention this to show, that God is still just what the late Mr George Muller proved Him to be, in a most signal manner—" The living and true God," who hears and answers prayer. Such an experience is a great stimulant to faith.

We then searched for a more suitable spot, and seeing an old coloured man sitting in front of his little room, mending a pair of boots, we asked if he knew of a piece of ground near the railway, where we might erect a large Gospel Tent. The old man cast his eyes around him, and at once suggested a spot right before us. We examined the place, and found it most suitable; nicely sheltered from the winds. How wonderful! Here, only fifty yards from the railway station, was God's appointed place for our tent, which became the spiritual birthplace of not a few souls; five or six of them from one family alone.

I might mention another instance of God's dealings with us. We erected the tent in a village just outside Cape Town, right in the heart of the strong south-easterly gales, and three times it came down whilst we were there. The second time was on a Lord's Day evening, just as we were about to light our lamps, with a big crowd of people outside waiting to come in. But nothing could be done to keep it standing. Oh! what a business, in the face of a raging gale, and fourteen or fifteen bags of sawdust, together with sand, blinding one! "What shall we do with the people?" asked an anxious lady, living near. "Pack them into your house, and we will be there as soon as possible," was the reply. And with some willing hands, we soon had the tent under control. Now a wash to get some of the sand and sawdust out of our eyes and ears, all the while looking to God for a message. We got " They sought means to bring him in, and to lay him before Him." " That will do " was the heart's response. We came downstairs, and found the room and passage full of people. I took the first part of the Service; my brother followed. At the close, one dear woman sitting on my right was definitely saved. Such happenings could be multiplied, but I must forbear, and only mention one more instance in our tent experience. On hearing of the intention of the Government to extend the railway from Kalk Bay to Simonstown, we decided to take the tent and pitch it in the midst of seven to eight hundred men. This we did, right between two big mountains, where the good seed was sown nightly, both in English and in Dutch, for two months.

At this time there was no Gospel testimony connected with the small assembly in Cape Town, consequently two leading brethren waited upon my brother and I, to ascertain " If a Gospel Service was begun, would one of us make it a point to be there ? " After a little consultation, we promised that one or the other of us, would go up to Cape Town every Lord's Day, which meant remaining over until Monday, and leaving only one at the tent. It so happened one Lord's Day, that it was my turn to remain, and about 7 p.m. I was just entering to light the lamps, when suddenly a great gust of wind came down between the mountains, lifting the tent completely off the ground, carrying everything before it, and, but for

GOSPEL TENT WORK IN SOUTH AFRICA

heavy boulders to which extra strainers were fastened, I don't know what might have become of it. Within half an hour, it was pouring heavy rain. I was most anxious to have the tent under control, lest it should tear to pieces. Knowing of a Christian connected with the South African General Mission, who was working further along the line, I sought if possible to get his assistance. On arriving at his little tent, I found him holding a Service with a few men. Having explained to him my difficulty, he at once brought his Service to a close, and suggested to the men that " they should go along and help Brother Fish." And so right here, we have the comforting words of the wise man "A brother is born for adversity" (Dutch, *in* adversity). We were soon on the spot, and in quick time got the tent under control, and at 2 a.m. we were there in our little bell tent, drinking coffee and singing hymns.

And so I might go on to tell of two years' most happy and successful service in the tent, though we were not without our trials ; having to contend with strong S.E. winds which prevail there during the summer months. Many a time we had the unpleasant experience of seeing our tent blown down. Still we can testify to God's glory, that never on one single occasion did we erect that tent, without souls being saved. The tent was subsequently sent to Johannesburg, where it was used to advantage by our beloved brother, Mr James F. Goch, until it was quite worn out.

Now the foregoing is a sort of introduction, and will serve as a link to the following detailed account

ROBBEN ISLAND

of our periodical visits to Robben Island Asylum, throughout the past thirty-four years.

If any attempt to put into shape and bring together the items embraced in these brief notes (made at the time of our visits), serve the object in view, namely God's glory, and the encouragement of His dear people, in this work, then the writer will have been amply rewarded.

But in approaching such a task, I feel most keenly, not only my utter unworthiness, but also my personal insufficiency to relate what *the Lord* has been doing throughout those busy years.

CHAPTER VII.

OUR FIRST VISIT TO ROBBEN ISLAND.

At the close of 1889, in the month of September, my brother and I made our first visit to the Robben Island Institute, together with a few Christian friends.

There were at that time from 50 to 100 leper patients on the island, living in long, low-roofed, corrugated-iron sheds, which during the summer months were unbearably hot, and this together with the unpleasant effluvia arising from the diseased bodies made it anything but a desirable sphere to labour in.

However, God's Grace was sufficient for the work then, and has been ever since.

For from two to three years, we only visited the island occasionally. In the meantime I had married the only daughter of the late J. W. van der Rijst, so that my path, in some respects was naturally diverted from my brother's. However, we still continued in our service together as much as possible, especially in visiting the poor lepers on Robben Island.

I might mention just here, that in the middle of the year 1892, a large Exhibition was about to be held in Kimberley, lasting over four months.

My brother and I, feeling that this would be an

ROBBEN ISLAND

unique opportunity to witness for the Lord, decided to go up, taking with us a good quantity of tracts.

On our arrival there, we were met by Mr Thos. Winship, who is at the present time a Registered Accountant in Durban, Natal.

Mr Winship very kindly found us suitable accommodation, and for four or five months we enjoyed happy fellowship together in the service of the Lord.

We were kept busy every day distributing tracts among the people, and entering into conversation with all who were prepared to listen to us.

A very interesting account of our visit here might be given if space would permit.

Towards the close of the Exhibition, my dear wife joined me in Kimberley, and after remaining for about a month, we both returned to our home in Wynberg, my brother continuing here for about a year.

From this time onward, I took up work among the lepers more definitely, and, in dependence upon God, have endeavoured to visit them once a week, sometimes twice, ever since.

In this most trying work, one's faith has been tested time and again. But looking back over the past thirty-four years, we can raise our "Ebenezer" and say, "Hitherto hath the Lord helped us."

For a considerable time, the sight of these poor corrupting bodies, and the effluvia from the most loathsome disease, was a trial to me, being naturally very sensitive to these things. Still, we can bless God for all the experiences one has had, and magnify His wondrous Grace, which we have proved to be more than sufficient for our need.

OUR FIRST VISIT TO ROBBEN ISLAND

Many a sad heart has been made to rejoice, many a drooping spirit revived, as we have told out the message of the Cross of Christ.

Thank God, that message can do for man, what nothing else in the whole world can.

During these years, I have visited the Transvaal four or five times, but in my absence have had the satisfaction of knowing that the poor lepers were being visited occasionally by my brother, Joseph.

Subsequently, he was engaged in Bible Carriage work, for a few years, and visited many parts of the Colony. If I remember rightly, he made his last tour, at the close of the Boer War. Thus the Word of God, as well as many Gospel books, especially *Grace and Truth* (in Dutch), were spread abroad. In the meantime, I was able to continue my weekly visits to the island alone, but up to 1896, I kept no record or detailed account of them.

I preserve this simple *Diary* form of our visits and service for the Lord among the lepers there, in order to engage the sympathies and the fellowship in prayer of Christian readers, the wide world over, for the lepers of Robben Island, and the spread of God's Gospel among them.

CHAPTER VIII.

EIGHT DAYS WITH THE LEPERS.

1896.—The following account of an eight-day's visit to Robben Island, has been written, with a view of drawing out the hearts of God's people in sympathy and prayer for those dear lepers.

Monday, 20th January.—Mr Jas. F. Goch and I left for the island, for the purpose of holding a series of Gospel Services, amongst the patients.

Monday evening, 8 to 9, at our first Service, about a hundred were present. Mr Goch spoke in Dutch, from Luke xix. 3. "And he sought to see Jesus who He was." We had a very precious time, and felt much of the Lord's presence.

Tuesday, 11 to 12 a.m.—We held a meeting for the women; about sixty were present. The same Scriptures were read, and we had a very profitable time. Two or three lepers who were anxious, were spoken to after this meeting.

3.30 to 4.30.—A meeting for the men was next held, about thirty being present. Mr Goch spoke again, from Luke xv., "The Lost Sheep," and I closed in prayer. A few were personally spoken to, at the conclusion of the meeting.

Evening, 8 to 9. Lantern Service.—Mr Goch explained with much liberty each picture as it was thrown upon the sheet, and was enabled by God's

EIGHT DAYS WITH THE LEPERS

help to bring out the Gospel most clearly. The room was packed with patients, and some of the island officials were also present.

What a sight! one not soon to be forgotten! Not less than two hundred poor disfigured faces, some of them beaming with the joy of the Lord! The Superintendent, who was present, said that he was convinced that these meetings were already having a " good effect " upon the people.

Wednesday, 11 a.m. to noon.—A meeting for the women. Spoke from Luke xv., " Lost and Found." About sixty attended, several showed signs of repentance, and expressed their desire to be saved; a few were spoken to at the close of the Service.

3.30 to 4.30.—Meeting for the men at which Mr Goch spoke from Gen. iii. We then went to the female wards, and held a short Service for them. Then our Lantern Service, which was the crowning one for the day. Imagine if you can such, a sight! Old and young, working their way into the room, some limping, others crawling, having neither hands nor feet, and with frightfully disfigured faces! In a very short time about two hundred were packed together, eager to hear God's message of love.

They were asked first to sing two or three of their favourite hymns, which they did most charmingly. I must confess that as I stood upon the table passing the slides, my heart was melted, under a sense of the great privilege of being allowed to minister God's glad tidings to these poor outcasts. Dear Mr Goch, spoke with great liberty from the " Prodigal Son." One very old blind woman of eighty years, a believer, could not sleep that night, but like Paul and Silas, between one and two in the morning, "prayed and sang praises to God."

Thursday.—Another meeting with the women this morning. Spoke from Gen. xix. and 2 Peter iii. About fifty present. After dinner we had a men's meeting, a goodly number attending, and we felt the presence of the Lord very specially. Later, we had another Lantern Service, this time amongst the women, the place being packed.

Friday, 11 to 12.—Again a goodly gathering of the women; one dear girl professed to be saved, and others showed signs of repentance and soul anxiety. In the afternoon, a much larger number of men came together, and it was evident that God was working in the hearts of some. Oh! for patience to allow God to do His own blessed work, in His own time, and in His own way!

> "Blind unbelief is sure to err,
> And scan His work in vain.
> God is His own interpreter,
> And He will make it plain."

Some of His own have been much encouraged, and they tell us that it has been a blessed week, one never to be forgotten. We had our usual Lantern Service, about two hundred and fifty men and boys sat on the floor and listened with rapt attention whilst each view was shown and explained. What a heart-melting time it was! What a picture! Answering fully to Isa. i. 6, "Wounds, bruises, and putrifying sores"; it was most inspiring to listen to the hearty

EIGHT DAYS WITH THE LEPERS

singing; the very place seemed to tremble. God grant that this Service may bear fruit in the lives of all who were present.

Saturday.—We filled in the time to-day by holding a few meetings for men and women, and visiting many who were confined to bed.

Lord's Day.—We spent most of the morning in meditation of the Word. Afternoon, a Service for the men, a hundred being present; subject, "The Coming of the Lord." Later, a meeting with the women, and again in the evening a gathering for the women, one hundred and twenty attending. The singing in English, Dutch, and Kaffir was deeply impressive; tears flowing freely down the poor disfigured faces! At the close, many expressed their deep gratitude for the blessing they had received during this special effort.

One man said that he was now forty years old, but had never heard such things before. Our visit seems to have changed the very atmosphere of the Island; one can understand it more or less, it being the first time that anything of the sort has been attempted here.

Monday.—We held our farewell meeting for the women, a hundred being present. It was very touching, many being in tears. I would rather watch any other person weep than see tears run down the face of a poor leper, for, to say the least, it is a most pitiable sight. On our return, we met many of the dear men, also weeping, and expressing their gratitude for our visit to the Island. One dear believer told us, that in a dream a little while back, he had seen two

ROBBEN ISLAND

men coming to the island to preach the Gospel, and the moment we entered the ward : " There ! " said he, " are the two men." The joy of the Lord filled his soul.

A very remarkable patient, who has only been a few months on the Island, and whom we visited several times, is a man who was Station-Master at one of the up-country stations. On rising one morning, he was alarmed somewhat by noticing some brown patches on his arms. Feeling his eyes a bit stiff, he went to the mirror, and to his astonishment found that his face was the same. A doctor was called, and yet another, until no less than five doctors had seen him, and after holding a consultation they decided that he was a *pronounced leper*.

Now this man knew well, that according to the Government Segregation Act, he would be compelled to go to the island, and knowing this, he determined not to be taken out of his own house alive. In this state of mind he resolved to take his own life. He made one or two attempts which failed, finally trying to shoot himself. This too, actually failed, and just in that extreme moment of distress, God met him and stopped his madness. Oh ! what a God of mercy ! And now as a broken man, he saw, not only his own guilt, but the Hand of God's mercy restraining him from that rash act.

It is interesting to know, that a Christian lady with whom I was acquainted, also in the Government Service, hearing of his illness, wrote him, expressing her sympathy with him, and pointing him to Christ the only true source of comfort. This timely

EIGHT DAYS WITH THE LEPERS

letter of condolence, was used of God in a most signal manner, and as a contrite man, I met him on Robben Island for the first time.

It was really wonderful to listen to him, as with eyes filled with tears, he told how God met with him.

On one occasion he said that he had nearly broken his neck over God's intervening hand. He says also, that " he would rather live on Robben Island with his terrible affliction, but knowing Christ as his Saviour, than possess the worth of twenty of the towns in which he had lived previously without Christ." Such is the power of a true conversion on one who has new life in Christ in his soul !

CHAPTER IX.

THE LOVE OF CHRIST CONSTRAINETH.

11th March 1896.—I felt unwell this morning; my dear wife seeing this, suggested that I should remain at home and not go to the island. But feeling specially constrained to go, I went. On my arrival there, I was asked by the aforementioned man to call and see two of the male patients in No. 1 Ward. Finding them a little anxious regarding their souls, I sought to make the Gospel very clear to them. One of the two was a poor humble Kaffir, badly afflicted, known as Sammy. The other was an Afrikander who is evidently drawing near his end. To him also, I spoke plainly of Christ and His atoning death, but I fear he was too weak to grasp it; the other, however, was led to trust the Saviour. Oh, that the love of Christ, in all its constraining warmth and power, may be known in my soul, and that I may "so speak" (Acts xiv. 1), that many, very many, of those poor lepers may be truly saved.

18th March.—Thanks be to Him who has permitted me to visit the dear lepers once more. On my arrival this morning, I learned that one of the two spoken to last week, the Africander, had passed away. Whether he died in peace or not, no one could tell me, but the reality of Sammy's conversion was quite evident

THE LOVE OF CHRIST CONSTRAINETH

after a further conversation with him. He is still very weak, and apparently not long for this world.

28*th March.*—Fine weather to-day, with the exception of a slight swell from south-west. Arrived in good time, was soon in my old quarters; had a talk with some patients on the way to the wards, of that theme of above themes. Saw Lm., who seemed fairly well. Went to No. 1. On entering, my eyes were at once turned towards the bed whereon Sammy a week before lay, but the poor disfigured face was no longer to be seen. Sammy was " with the Lord, which is very far better." Spent the remainder of my time in No. 3 Ward.

1*st April.*—Took a company of young people across to-day from Dalgosafat, who had long expressed their desire to visit the leper patients. My dear wife, Ethel, and Miss Clark, were among the number. I was able to take them through all the wards, which had an exceedingly touching affect. The weather was fine going to the island, but terribly rough returning. The boat pitched heavily, and many of the passengers were ill.

15*th April.*—Another eight-days' visit to the island with Mr Jas F. Goch and Mr E. Tapson.

It was with much joy that we left Wynberg, and on arrival, at once set to work to arrange meetings. After consulting the Commissioner, seeing the Doctor and Dutch Reformed Minister, our path seemed clear to make a commencement, thus proving the truth of Prov. xxi. 1, " The king's heart is in the hand of the Lord, as the rivers of water, He turneth it whithersoever He will."

ROBBEN ISLAND

We had our first meeting among the men, from 5 to 6 p.m., a hundred and twenty present, who listened with rapt attention to the story of the Cross told by Mr Jas. Goch. Mr Tapson assisted with the harmonium, while several Dutch hymns were sung.

Again, what a sight for human eyes to behold! Old and young making their way to the meeting, some crawling, others shuffling in a most painful manner on their backs, whilst perhaps the most touching scene of all was a man with neither hands or feet, being borne on the shoulders of another. Thus we found ourselves in the midst of a motley crowd, corresponding very much to Luke's picture—" *Poor, maimed,* and *halt,* and *blind.*"

Saturday, 7th.—Mr Tapson and I were early at the Wards this morning, arranging for meetings for the day, and we did also a little visiting. First meeting, from 11 to 12—a good number present. After dinner, arranged slides for Lantern Service. A meeting commenced at 5.15 p.m.—went on till 8 o'clock, with half an hour of interval. The room was crowded to excess. Once more a sight surpassing all others, for human sympathy!

As I stood upon that table passing the slides, my tears would flow. Around me on every side were precious souls whose bodies were decaying away; yet for such, the eternal Son of God left the glory, and died upon the tree; all in order that poor despised creatures such as these, might share in His glory. It brought before me most vividly the scene of two years before, when we stood there under the same sort of circumstances, but alas! no less than two

THE LOVE OF CHRIST CONSTRAINETH

hundred had passed into eternity since then. To where?

Sunday, 17th.—Had a very precious meeting with the men this morning. And at the close of the Service, one dear man came forward saying, he desired to be saved. We spoke to him for some time, and after a little, perhaps, undue pressure, he professed to be saved. He was present again in the evening, and when asked if he was fully trusting in Jesus he said, " You pressed me this morning to give an answer, but it was not until after, when by my own bedside, that I considered the matter, and that I was able clearly to see the truth. And now I feel like a candle drawn out of a mould "; he meant to say that it was no patched-up business, but that the work was *real*; he was a *new man*. This was the first case of conversion, on this occasion.

We went to the women's quarters and found a goodly number waiting to listen to the message of the Cross.

Although Mr Goch gave an earnest word, yet there was not the manifest breaking down, which we were eagerly looking for.

Monday, 18th.—We did some visiting among the men this morning, and found five or six anxious about their souls. Had a service for the natives later, and, after dinner, Mr Tapson and I again visited amongst the men, afterwards going to Murray's Bay (the female Wards), to make arrangements for the Lantern Service. In the meantime, Mr Goch had an earnest word with four women in Miss D's. room, and the result was, that one professed salvation. Again we

ROBBEN ISLAND

had a most touching Service, the place being packed with women and girls. The Service was held in Dutch and Kaffir, with hearty singing in both languages.

Tuesday, 19th.—Mr Tapson and I were early at the Wards this morning. Mr Goch remained at our rooms, selecting slides for the Evening Service. We visited No. 1 Ward later, and held a Service in No. 2.

Mr Goch and I then went to No. 3 Ward, and saw Botha, who, after being dealt with very faithfully, definitely received Christ. Mr Tapson and I returned to our quarters, Mr Goch going on to the females. We sought the Lord earnestly for the Evening Service, and were full of expectation. We continued our visiting on our way to the females, where again we experienced much of the Lord's presence; God graciously stretching out His hand and delivering souls.

At the close, Mr Tapson and I were asked to hold a Service in English for the Nurses, which we did, in their large waiting room.

Wednesday, 20th.—We did some visiting, then held a Service in No. 6 Ward; after the meeting, spoke to a few who professed to be saved. It was now evident to us that God was working. We continued our work of visiting, and held the Evening Service in No. 2. Mr Goch spoke very earnestly; I then followed with a brief word in Dutch. It was an interesting meeting, one dear man who had trusted Christ that day, saying at the close that "he had received Him with *both* his hands."

In the morning a poor woman came to us weeping

THE LOVE OF CHRIST CONSTRAINETH

and sobbing aloud, confessing herself a lost sinner, and saying that she was afraid God would cast her off for ever. How precious His Word, " I will in no wise cast out."

Thursday, 21st, 11 a.m.—Mr Tapson spoke in English, Mr Goch interpreted, and I closed the meeting with a word in Dutch. Continued our visiting after dinner, and held a Service for the women, a good number being present.

Friday, 22nd.—We held two farewell meetings to-day, one for the men and one for the women. There were many longing faces as we bade them farewell.

There are several little trollies running on a narrow line down the Island, and these were crowded with men, women, and children, singing out in Dutch, that well-known old Revival Hymn :

" O, the Lamb, the bleeding Lamb, the Lamb upon Calvary,
The Lamb that was slain, and liveth again, to intercede for me."

Our visit was crowned by a fine passage back, and, above all, we have the satisfaction of knowing that no less than eighteen poor lepers had professed to be saved that day. Glorious grace !

12th May.—I have been prevented from going to the island for the past three weeks, having so much to do, and the weather has been frequently stormy. I met with several little groups of men outside the Wards this morning and found them quite prepared to listen to the Word. Later on, I went to No. 3 Ward, where I had a nice time with Botha, Smidt, and another young man ; the two former, I believe, are

ROBBEN ISLAND

truly saved. I read several passages bearing on the assurance of salvation. It is just here, where so many of them are lacking in understanding. I told them that the best preachers on Robben Island were those whose lives testified to the truth they spoke, *i.e.*—the best "walkers." Read 2 Cor. iv. to a dear old believer, afterwards went along to the females. But my time being limited, I did not get beyond Mrs Ls. and Miss D.

Dear old Mrs E. passed away last Monday, very quietly. She was a poor wavering soul; I hope, however, that she is with the Lord.

20*th May.*—It has been a perfect sea to-day, calm and cool; we reached the Island in good time, so that by 11 a.m. I was in the Wards. In No. 1, I read a few passages to a poor fellow who was almost suffocated; he appeared to be much comforted. I then passed on to Goosen's bed. He is also a believer. After speaking to him on the assurance of God's salvation, I asked him the question: " Did he believe that he would some day die ? " " Oh, yes," said he, " that is one thing I am certain of." I again asked if he were quite sure of his salvation. " Oh yes," with emphasis. " Let us look at the Scriptures," said I, " and hear what they say about it." After reading a few passages and long before I had finished speaking, the dear man's face was all aglow with joy, " Oh, that's precious, sir, how very plain."

Called at No. 6 Ward, but my heart was made sad when speaking to four or five scoffers. One said that he would rather die, than remain on that Island, for then his soul would go to heaven. I asked him

THE LOVE OF CHRIST CONSTRAINETH

if he was certain of that, " Yes," said he, " where do you think I should go to—in the air ? " " No, but unless you are born again you can never enter into the Kingdom of God, and if you die in your sins you will surely go to Hell." " There is no Hell." " Oh ! said I, is that it ? " " Sir, have you ever seen Hell ? " " Yes, I said." " Have you ever been there ? " " No, no, but I see it in this Book," holding up my Bible. " Oh, that's nothing." " I thought you told me a moment ago that your soul would go to heaven if you died ? Pray tell me how you happen to know that there is a heaven ? " " I read it in the Bible." " Well ! that seems strange that you can believe in the reality of one place, because the Bible says so, and not in the other of which the Bible also speaks." After a word of warning, I left them.

26th May.—Had a very profitable time with Mr Lm. over three remarkable expressions of the Apostle Paul's, " The least of the Apostles " (1 Cor. xv. 9) ; " Though I be nothing " (2 Cor. xii. 11) ; " Chief of Sinners " (1 Tim. i. 15).

3rd June.—Met Mr Tapson this morning, on his arrival from Johannesburg. He went with me to the Island. We saw Mr Lm., who appears to be more humble now. We had a good time in No. 1 Ward. One man told us that he had been brought to the Lord since our recent visit to the Island. Outside No. 2 Ward, we had a profitable time with Stephanes and several others, who have quite recently been saved, before passing on to No. 3 Ward. In No. 6 Ward, we also had a refreshing time. Mr Tapson said, " We could not pass you by." " Yes," replied one ;

"it is so like Jesus, who in order to meet with a poor woman, went a long way round. So you, too, had to come this way, to give us a comforting word." Mr Tapson remarked that God loves His children greatly, and is waiting to have them home with himself, but there are others to be saved. "Yes," said he, "Jonah was angry because the gourd withered away, but he had no pity for the thousands of souls in Nineveh, who knew not their right hand from their left." Had a little word with Mrs Ls., and Miss D. Found Miss de K. in her room very ill. On entering, she expressed her joy at seeing us again. Mr Tapson commenced to speak about the Word, but was soon interrupted by an outburst of "Oh! God has answered my prayer in sending you to me to-day; I have been praying and longing to see you both." "Have you been longing to see us?" asked Mr Tapson. "Yes, why should I not long to see you my friends? Oh, God has been teaching me. I have said to you many times, Mr Fish, that I never would tell you what was in my heart, but God has given me my desire in seeing you again." "That is very nice indeed," I said, "but the great burden of my heart has been that you might see Jesus, and receive Him as your Saviour." "Oh, yes, He is my Saviour, and I am saved, and now I long to see my nurse saved." I had pleaded hard with the Lord for this dear girl; all along, she persistently refused to listen to the Word, but by long and earnest prayer the stony heart had been softened, and now we have had the joy of seeing her trusting in the Lord.

16th June.—Had the pleasure of my brother

THE LOVE OF CHRIST CONSTRAINETH

Joseph's company to-day. Sea fairly smooth, but an unpleasant swell on the beach. This primitive way of being carried on the shoulders of natives and landed on the beach, is not always a very enjoyable experience ; especially if the said native happens to get his legs entangled in the seaweed, and dumps you down head first into the water. Such an enjoyable(?) bath I had one morning ! and to make matters worse, they dressed me up in a suit of white clothes, about three sizes too big for me. This is only one way, God has of cooling our pride. And through His mercy, I was none the worse for my involuntary bath.

We found Miss de K. very weak and a little deranged in mind, but she brightened considerably by our visit.

We saw the Commissioner with reference to a free tea for all the patients. He was very pleased, and gave his consent readily.

2nd July 1898.—My brother and I were again on the Island, and arranged to give the tea, next week. One fresh patient was taken over to-day. There are now 320 male, and 223 female patients in the Institution.

11th July.—Last Saturday, Joseph and I went over and remained on the Island until Monday. We should have gone on Thursday, but were prevented by the weather.

On Saturday, we gave the women their tea. About a hundred and twenty gathered in No. 5 Ward, and we spoke to them for one hour " of the good things to come," reminding them of " the durable riches, and of the bread that perisheth not." We then proceeded to another Ward, where a similar number were assembled, and we spoke to them for an hour also. It was a real joy to our hearts to see these poor afflicted creatures so happy. Oh! that many of them may soon possess that " blessing which maketh rich, and to which no sorrow is added."

On Lord's Day, we gave the men their tea, holding Services amongst them.

On Monday we were very busy cutting up over 1000 yards of flannelette, and distributing it among the women.

25th July.—To-day we had the joy of speaking to many, some individually, some in small groups, just as we found them about the Island. One woman we spoke to, was deeply troubled about her soul, and I am sure that she will have no rest, until she accepts Him, " whom to know is life eternal." Oh, that His Word may go forth with mighty quickening power, that their dead souls may hear His voice and live!

8th August.—Unable to get over last Friday, it being too stormy. Even to-day, it is by no means pleasant—this is our most stormy month—great precaution being necessary in landing passengers, as there was a heavy sea running at the Jetty. The Government have at last succeeded in making a Jetty at the Island, and it is proving a boon to all concerned.

Our sister, Miss D., is confined to bed and suffering considerably. (She was at one time in one of the Assemblies on the mainland). Truly leprosy is no respecter of persons; rich and poor, old and young alike, become victims to it. Dear Old Mrs A. is as bright as ever, although stone blind. Amongst others

THE LOVE OF CHRIST CONSTRAINETH

to whom we spoke in the same Ward, was a young girl, much disfigured. She appeared very weak, and not yet saved. Oh, how helpless one feels at times, in dealing with such souls! Well may we say with one of old, " If the Lord do not help thee, whence shall I help thee ? (2 Kings vi. 27).

15th August.—I was alone—yet not alone—to-day, my brother being unwell. Called and saw Mr Lm.; thence, after a little conversation, went to No. 1, where I had much joy in speaking to several confined to bed. Went to Murray's Bay, and gave the remainder of my time to Mrs Ls and Miss D., explaining several passages of Scripture, which, I must confess, were also very refreshing to my own soul. And so we find His Word ever true ; " The liberal soul shall be made fat, and he that watereth, shall be watered also himself " (Prov. xi. 25).

22nd August.—Our hearts were saddened as we boarded the boat this morning, to find Mr de V., with his poor afflicted daughter, going to the Island, where her mother already is. Poor girl! A fine young lady of twenty-five summers, and about to be married. Tears flowed freely as we sought to comfort her. She might well have said with Job of old: " Miserable comforters are ye all " (Job xvi. 2). Who but our blessed Lord can fully sympathise with these sad outcasts ? He alone can dry the weeping eye, and comfort the sorrowing heart.

> " His purposes will ripen fast,
> Unfolding every hour ;
> The bud may have a bitter taste,
> But sweet will be the flower."

ROBBEN ISLAND

This is the *third* one afflicted in this family. One died recently, and the mother's mind became affected through grief. After a good passage, we soon found ourselves in our old quarters, following our Lord's example, *i.e.* " preaching glad tidings to the poor, binding up the broken-hearted," etc.

We had interesting talks with some believers. One old man said that " he wished he could get such seasons of refreshing every day, for it was strength and courage to his soul."

I heard to-day of one man who disguised himself sufficiently to escape from the Island, actually coming back on the boat with the passengers.

29th August.—Mr Goodman, late of London, went over with me to-day. I was able to take him through many Wards, thus giving him a little idea of the work, but not knowing Dutch, he was at a disadvantage.

23rd September.—Sorry to find Mr Lm. in bed with influenza. Read John, chap xiii., and referred to the work of intercession, reminding him of the three letters P : " Saved from the *Penalty* of Sin by His death ; Saved from the *Power* of Sin by His life ; and Saved from the *Presence* of Sin at His coming, to fetch us away." Visited several in No. 1, one man being definitely helped. Went to Murray's Bay, but did not remain long with Mrs Ls., her husband being over. Had an earnest word with Miss de V.

15th November.—I have not been able to cross to the Island for the past seven weeks, owing to illness, but I am glad that my brother has been able to carry on the work in the meantime. Some of the patients were overjoyed to see me again, and it was no less a

THE LOVE OF CHRIST CONSTRAINETH

joy to me to visit them once more. On nearing No. 1, I met the Superintendent, who asked me to speak to a poor fellow who was very near his end, but before I could approach his bed a quantity of eucalyptus oil had to be sprinkled round and on his bed. Even then the effluvium arising from his body was almost unbearable. The Doctor said : " the inside is entirely rotted away." To watch a poor leper dying, is one of the most touching sights in the whole world. Afterwards I went to the female Wards, and found Mrs Ls. very weak. I think she is sinking.

23rd November.—There are indications of a storm this morning, a heavy sea running. Saw Mr Lm., but he was in a state of great anxiety regarding his wife who was ill.

The man whom I spoke to in No. 1 last week, and who was so ill, died the next day, but before he passed away he sent for his friends in No. 3, and as they stood round his bed he told them of the " peace " he had with God, and whilst in the act of pointing upwards, and saying, " I am going there," he fell asleep. " Blessed sleep, from which none ever wake to weep."

I called again at Lm.'s room, and found him weeping. He had just received a cable to say that his wife was dying. In the midst of his sorrows, he realised that " The Father of mercies, and the God of all comfort was near him."

Seven lepers went over to-day, three males and four females, two being man and wife.

29th November.—On arriving at the island this morning, I saw lying on the beach a large shark

ROBBEN ISLAND

which the fishermen had caught during the night. It was twelve feet long and very thick. Alongside it were six full-sized seals which had been taken out of its stomach.

Mr Lm. was still in a state of anxiety concerning his wife, although they say that she is a little better. Had a nice time with some natives in No. 4, and also a profitable time with the women.

13th December.—It was too stormy to get across last week. Mr Lm. was rejoicing this morning having received news of his wife's recovery. Visited Nos. 1 and 2 Wards, also Murray's Bay in the afternoon. Mrs Ls. was a little better, but Miss D. much worse, in fact too ill to be seen.

Five fresh cases were taken to the island to-day, making 350 male and 230 female patients there now.

10th March 1899.—I have been absent, in Johannesburg, for eight weeks. During my stay there, Brother Jas. F. Goch and I visited the two leper locations outside of Pretoria. We hired a cab one fine morning, put as many water melons as possible into it, and started for the most distant Institute, six and a half miles out, where we found 130 native patients, men, women, and children, huddled together in tents and huts,—but this we learned was only a temporary arrangement, until large, commodious buildings could be erected. We soon gathered the poor lepers and spoke to them by means of interpreters. We had scarcely commenced our Service, when I noticed a little turtle dove perched upon the ridge of the hut right before us, where it remained the whole of the time. I felt deeply impressed by this incident, reminding me

THE LOVE OF CHRIST CONSTRAINETH

as it did, so forcibly of the Spirit of God brooding over this poor groaning, and suffering humanity. Thanks be to God, He has not left even the world without hope, for it shall one day " be delivered from the bondage of corruption, and be brought into the glorious liberty of the children of God " (Rom. viii. 21).

On our return we visited the smaller Institute, where we found thirty-five European patients, living in a most wretched condition, and we had a short Service with them also.

While in Johannesburg, I received a letter from Bath, making it possible for me to take a much-needed change to England. Personally I did not feel very anxious to go, but friends here urged me strongly to do so. And I yielded.

I returned almost immediately from the Transvaal to Wynberg, and continued my visits to the Island until the month of May, when my dear wife and I, with Miss Lorimer, my ward, left for England.

My brother kept visiting the lepers faithfully during my absence " up north." They were very glad to see me again. There is no service on earth more sweet to me, than this ministry to the lepers.

I was surprised when S. asked to-day that he might be received into fellowship. There was a time when he would not listen to the Word of God at all ; we only need a little patience to watch the effects of His Holy Word. " The husbandman waiteth for the precious fruit of the earth, and hath long patience for it " (Jas. v. 7-8).

27th March.—A nice time with Lm. to-day. Two men came to me whilst I was partaking of a little food

ROBBEN ISLAND

outside the Ward. One gets an experience of this sort now and again, reminding one of our Lord's great activities recorded by Mark: "There were many coming and going, and they had no opportunity so much as to eat." Thank God, we have no difficulty in getting a congregation on Robben Island; if we don't go to them, they will come to us.

I heard of a poor woman who died this week. It is said that the stench from her body was so terrible, that the other patients in the same Ward could not endure it. She was then placed in a bathroom adjoining the Ward, but even then, the offensive odour was unbearable. At last she was removed outside altogether, where, after a few days lingering she died. They placed her body quickly into a coffin, and buried it out of sight. "Oh, my God, is this a picture of sin? If so, I am humbled in the dust before Thee."

5th April.—Miss Walker and Miss Belsland went with me to-day, and were much affected by what they saw. Poor S. was still in the body, but suffering terribly. All his face from his forehead down to his mouth is clean gone; it was almost impossible to come near him. Mrs Ls. was very weak, obliged to have all the windows and doors wide open to get air; with tears she earnestly asked the prayers of God's children. Oh, what a trial to the flesh, soon to pass away and leave those three sweet little children to live and die as lepers on that island. Thank God she knows Him who came "to bind up the broken heart and to comfort all that mourn" (Isaiah lxi. 1). She came from a wealthy European family, and was the wife of a well-to-do farmer.

THE LOVE OF CHRIST CONSTRAINETH

14*th April.*—I was accompanied to-day by Brother Lennox, late of Ireland, who was deeply moved by the pitiable sights he saw. We spoke mostly to believers. Dear Mrs Ls. is very weak, Miss D. also; poor S. to my great surprise is still in the body.

28th *April.*—Dear Mrs Ls., fell asleep last Saturday, after months of severe suffering. Many of the women are mourning her loss, for she was a true friend to them all, but no one will feel her loss more than Miss D. The evening before she fell asleep, she sat up in bed, but her aunt, who was with her—also a leper—told her that she " must lie down and take her rest." " Yes," she said, " but I am going to my eternal rest, and in the morning I shall be with my Jesus." " Blessed hope, blessed rest for my soul." Miss D. says : " I do feel her loss sadly, but whatever God does, is right."

Poor S. is too weak to take any nourishment, and is dying.

Had a profitable time with several patients.

Oh, what an unspeakable privilege to be allowed of God to visit these lepers, and tell them of Jesus.

I am now about leaving for England, and expect to be absent not less than six months. It is hard to part with the dear lepers, not knowing that I shall ever meet some again. My brother is not working his Bible Carriage just now, and has promised to continue his visits to the Island.

[My dear wife and I left for England in May 1899, and were away over a year. During our absence, war was declared between England and the Transvaal, and on our return in June 1900, I took up the work

ROBBEN ISLAND

at the docks—single-handed—of meeting the transports on their arrival from England. This service I continued for a year and nine months, without a break.]

s.s. *Moor*,
Lines written by J. W. Fish, after losing his passage in the Avondale Castle, *21st May* 1900.

Psalm xlvi. 10—

> " Be still," my child, thy path is known,
>   By Him who did it plan ;
> Who leads thee forth a second time,
>   To that fair distant land.
>
> " Be still," my child, and know 'tis God,
>   Who bids thee hasten forth ;
> The leper's cry is heard to-day,
>   "Come, tell us of God's love."
>
> " Be still," my child, and fear not aught,
>   Thy sorrowing heart to move ;
> The hand that guided in the past,
>   Will guide the future too.
>
> " Be still," my child, thy restless heart,
>   Is like the troubled sea ;
> Cast all thy burdens on the Lord,
>   Thou shalt sustainéd be.
>
> " Be still," my child, and rest upon,
>   My faithful written Word ;
> I ne'er have failed thee in the past,
>   " Thy exceeding great reward."
>
> " Be still," my child, for wisdom's path,
>   Is oft, in troubled sea ;
> But He who is " the God of peace,"
>   Thy perfect peace will be.
>
> " Be still," my child, and let no thought,
>   Of anxious care be thine ;
> The hand that guides thy little barque,
>   Works with His power Divine.

THE LOVE OF CHRIST CONSTRAINETH

> " Be still," my child, and know that thou,
>   Art kept by power Unseen ;
> The mind that's always stayed on *Me*,
>   Enjoys that peace serene.

> " Be still," my child, for yet, ere long,
>   Thy conflict will be o'er ;
> And then from sin and trial freed,
>   To love *Me* and adore.

> " Be still," my child, for soon the clouds,
>   Will burst in radiant sky ;
> That voice you'll hear with quickening shout,
>   Come reign *with Me* on high.

7th June 1900.—Returned from England, after an absence of over twelve months.

15th June.—Made my first visit to Robben Island to-day, since my return, accompanied by my brother, who has gone on faithfully with the work during my absence. The dear lepers were overjoyed to meet me once more. One poor fellow was so overcome with joy that he stretched out his poor arm—not a bit of hand—what could I do but shake it, even if I was running a risk!

22nd June.—A refreshing time with several of the believers to-day. Poor B. scarcely knew how to express his joy at meeting me again. We read the closing verses of 2 Cor. iv., and the opening verse of chapter v., pointing out the great difference between the coming of the Lord to the air for His saints, and " The day of the Lord " ; His coming to judge—truths which the Dutch people invariably confound.

Mrs M. is, without exaggeration, a pitiable object to behold ; her ears are four or five inches in length— more like dog's ears than those of a human being—

ROBBEN ISLAND

I knew her when she was a handsome young lady, but her face to-day, is more like the face of a lion, than anything else! All traces of those once beautiful features are gone! Still, she is happy in God's love. Oh, the triumphs of His wondrous Grace! She told a woman who died there this morning that: " If she could, she would take her place." The family never write or visit those afflicted daughters, in fact they refuse any longer to acknowledge them as their children. Oh, the stigma of this awful disease!

Poor Rosa S., who was so bright a year ago, is now a great sufferer; she, like many more here, has a silver tube inserted into her windpipe; her under lip projects at least two inches from her mouth; her hands are very bad, also her tongue is terrible to look at. She is a dear child of God, and wept copiously, not so much for sorrow as for joy, when I spoke to her of the blessed change that would take place at the coming of the Lord.

28th June.—Miss Watson and her niece from Belfast went over with me to-day. We passed through several Wards, speaking to one here and there, one woman professing to accept Christ. Poor Susanna S. was so bad that it was more than I could do to stand by her. Rosa is almost suffocated.

6th July.—On my arrival at the docks this morning, I met my brother's wife, who told me that Joseph had been left on the Island the day before. We had a good talk with Lm. about Church Truths. Had a good time in Wards 3 and 5, also a profitable time with Mrs M. and her sister Miss D.

20th July.—Brother Cameron and Brother Foster

THE LOVE OF CHRIST CONSTRAINETH

journeyed with me to-day. Both were deeply moved at the distressing sights, but thankful to see what Grace had wrought in the case of many. We had a nice time with the boys; dear Lukie Johnson, was again moved to tears. I said to him, " Lukie, what is your great difficulty, that you are not yet saved ? " " I can't see Jesus, sir." " Do you want to see Him, Lukie ? " " Yes, sir." " Well, Lukie, if you want to see Him by sight bye and bye, you must trust Him and look to Him by faith now."

Thirty-six fresh patients were sent to the Island this week. Thirty-five of them came from the Orange Free State, and one from Caledon, the latter leaving a wife and four children at home.

3rd August.—My ward, Miss Lorimer, accompanied me to-day, and we spent the whole of the day with the male patients. In No. 3, we witnessed a very touching scene. Poor Geldenhuis was anxious that I should pray for him, but whilst I was so engaged, a fit of suffocation overcame him, and it continued for at least an hour. He too, like so many, has a silver tube in his windpipe, and periodically this tube has to be cleared. It is most distressing to watch it being drawn out, as he does it, with a pair of scissors. Such may well take up the words of the Psalmist, and say : " How long wilt thou forget me ? For ever ? " (Psa. xiii. 1).

29th *August.*—To-day, Mr Peter Wilson, Mrs Mace, Mrs Joseph Fish, and Ethel went over. The three ladies went straight to the females, whilst Mr Wilson and I remained awhile amongst the men. Dear Brother Wilson could not restrain his tears, as he looked

ROBBEN ISLAND

upon some of these poor creatures, especially when I took him to see our sister Mrs M., who was very ill and troubled about losing her mind. " She would like to know if God would hold her responsible for anything that she said or did, whilst her mind was deranged." We sought to comfort her from the Word of God.

13th September.—I was alone again to-day. Found Mrs M. much better, God having heard our prayers on the previous visit. About a month ago, I was asked to speak to a man in No. 1 Ward, by name Andreas W., who was getting very weak. When I came to his bedside, he was lying with his head covered with the sheet. I called him by name, and, to my great astonishment, when he showed his face I found myself confronting one who had been the ringleader of much trouble on the island in the past, and who was one of five that escaped some time ago by means of a little boat they had made out of boxes, in a cave amongst the rocks. He was one of three who had been captured and brought back again. I had oftimes been insulted by him ; but here he was a dying man without Christ. I spoke kindly, but faithfully to him, from the Word of God. To-day, to my great joy, I found him much humbled, and resting on the finished work of Christ. Praise the Lord ! He assured me that his soul was truly saved, and that he knew that one day he would be in the Glory. This is another brand plucked from the fire (Zech. iii. 2).

29th September.—Mr Peter Wilson went with me again to-day. Andreas Williams and Geldenhuis, are both gone. Mr Lm. told us an interesting story

THE LOVE OF CHRIST CONSTRAINETH

regarding Andreas. He had often spoken to him about his soul, but he always abused him in return. He generally left him and told the Lord about it ; then returned to the attack the following day. One day he met Andreas outside the Ward, with his little cat following him. " Andreas," said he, " why does your cat follow you ? " " Because I am kind to it," was the reply. He asked him if people did not generally return kindness for kindness. " Yes," said he. " Then," said Mr Lm, " Jesus has been following you all your lifetime, and yet you drive Him from you."

This simple way of dealing with him seems to have had its desired effect (Pro. xxv. 15). Mr Lm. told us also of another man at whose house he called one day, and on hearing loud shouting he asked " Why are you making such a noise ? " " Oh," replied the man, " I never saw the love of Christ like this before. It is tremendous ! it is unspeakable ! " Mr Lm. thought he was wrong in his mind, but he assured him that it was not so. It reminds one of the words of Festus to Paul, " Thou art beside thyself ; much learning doth make thee mad " (Acts xxvi. 25). A day or two later, this one passed away, happy in the Lord.

10*th January* 1901.—Mr Crowhurst and I were over to-day ; we heard on our arrival that our dear sister Miss D. had passed away the night before, very peacefully.

This is the first visit I have made for more than three months, on account of small-pox being on the Island. It was very rough, and I did not feel well coming back. However, I went over again the follow-

ROBBEN ISLAND

ing day with my father-in-law, to conduct a funeral service.

29th August.—I have not been able to visit the poor lepers since last January on account of Bubonic Plague. We had a stormy passage, but reached the Island in safety. I felt quite moved to tears, on meeting the first leper. My thoughts ran back over twelve and a half years, when for the first time, I saw leprosy. Since then it has been my great privilege to visit those poor creatures hundreds of times. I found that many had passed away during the seven months; some to the bright regions above, others I fear, to the blackness of darkness forever. " Yet God willeth not the death of any man."

Dear Lm. is still bright and witnessing for the Lord.

Daniels and Arend are also shining brightly in the midst of the gloom on that poor, sorrow-stricken island. Little Lukie Johnson is very weak, but now happy in the knowledge of his sins forgiven.

CHAPTER X.

GOSPEL WORK DURING THE BOER WAR.

1902.—The Boer War has now been brought to a close, and I am not concerned about meeting details at the docks. For the past year and nine months, most of my time has been taken up in meeting transports with troops from England, distributing tracts and note-paper. Not less than 150,000 men have passed through my hands during that time. Many were spoken to personally, besides a Service for a large number when it was convenient. About 100,000 tracts and books were given away; about 30,000 sheets of note-paper and envelopes, besides a large amount of money collected from the men and sent to their friends. In addition to this, I have met a few thousand Boer prisoners in the Simonstown Camp, on their return to South Africa. The first batch I met was in August, 700 men from Peniche, Portugal; not less than 250 were brought to the Lord during their stay there. I usually worked among them in their little tents during the day, and sometimes was pressed to remain for an evening Service. At the first Service, 600 came together in a long corrugated-iron shed in the camp, where I preached the Gospel to them in Dutch. It was a most pathetic scene; quite a

ROBBEN ISLAND

number broke down into tears. Many of these poor fellows were returning, to find both wife and family all gone, having died in the concentration camps during their absence. One man professed to be saved through reading the Dutch edition of *God's Way of Salvation*.

18*th September.*—Visited the Boer camp again. There were 1000 Boer prisoners from Bermuda. I found several believers amongst them, who manifested a very subdued spirit; thank God.

16*th October.*—s.s. *Oritava* arrived with 1000 prisoners from St Helena, and came into the docks at Cape Town. I had two days amongst them, and took my father-in-law on board one evening to speak to them. It was grand to witness such a large number gathered on the poop-deck to listen to the Gospel in their mother tongue (Dutch).

7*th November.*—800 prisoners arrived to-day from St Helena. These, with another 1000 from Bermuda, who arrived also to-day, were all encamped together. The Commandant I met there, and found him very bright; he had been brought to the Lord whilst in Bermuda, through the instrumentality of Mr Sparrow, the English missionary who has long laboured there.

11*th November.*—I met 1000 from Ceylon to-day, there being some bright Christians among them; one of them a General. They told me that they had not heard the Gospel in their own tongue since they had been taken prisoners, and only had seven Dutch Bibles amongst the whole number. I sent them 100 Testaments the next morning.

30*th December.*—On visiting the Boer camp to-day,

GOSPEL WORK DURING THE BOER WAR

I found 900 men from India and had a hearty reception.

This is a most encouraging feature in the Dutch people. They are always prepared to listen to the Word of God.

8th January 1903.—Another 900 men from Ceylon were landed at Simonstown to-day. The blessing and presence of God amongst them was most manifest, such as I have not seen amongst any others whom I have met with yet. At their own request I remained for the evening, and held a Gospel Service, which was attended by a large number of attentive listeners.

31st *January*.—I met another 800 prisoners from Ceylon to-day, and had some very nice times amongst them, visiting the different tents and speaking to the men of Christ. I was asked to remain for an evening Service, but having other engagements could not do so.

During these four or five months, I have been able to distribute a few thousand pamphlets, *God's Way of Salvation*, in Dutch, and they will be read throughout the country. It is impossible to estimate the amount of blessing which will result therefrom. God Himself will see to that. I am reminded of the words in Eccl. xi. 6 : " In the morning sow thy seed, and in the evening withhold not thine hand."

12*th November*.—I went to the Island to-day, and had a nice word with Mr Lm. Poor old Silver seems happy in the Lord, but Oh, what an object of pity ! I cannot describe the condition of his body on paper. Another was " almost persuaded," to-day.

26*th November*.—Poor B. was very glad to see me. He is humbled and broken in the dust under the sense of his utter unworthiness before God. Now as a lost sinner, he claims the sinner's Saviour; "He came not to call the righteous but sinners to repentance."

My father-in-law went with me and we visited many of the Wards. It is sad to see so many young girls from twelve to twenty years of age afflicted. Eight were brought to the Island in one month. What a heavy Cross, just in the vigour of youth, to be banished to that Island, every hope dashed to the ground! Oh, for a grateful heart! Well may *we* sing—

> "What mercies He hath made me prove,
> His loving kindness, Oh, how good."

16th January 1903.—Glad of another opportunity to see the patients. At last I have succeeded in obtaining a Government standing Permit, to visit the lepers at any time. I had a very earnest conversation with one young man to-day.

30th *January*.—In speaking to James M., I was surprised to see the progress he had made in the knowledge of God's Word. He is a well educated young man, the eldest son of a Government contractor.

Poor B. His face is terribly swollen. I felt deeply for the poor fellow, still he is comforted knowing that his change will come some day.

I met a man in No. 3 Ward, just brought to the Island, leaving a sorrowing wife and child on the mainland; they cannot get him to eat or speak. I fear his mind has become weak, yet it is remarkable that as soon as I began to speak and read to him from the Word of God, he was stirred and spoke freely,

GOSPEL WORK DURING THE BOER WAR

although with tears. What a vale of tears we are in ! " The whole creation groaneth together in pain until now, waiting for the adoption, to wit the redemption of the body." Blessed hope for the child of God. " Behold, I come quickly," Amen, even so, Come, Lord Jesus (Rev. xxii. 20).

Lines suggested on the return journey of Mr James Fish, after ten years' labour for the Lord in South Africa.

> " The Avondale Castle," God speed on her way,
> And guard her from peril by night and by day,
> Let winds shew Thy favour, and waters declare,
> Thy marvellous kindness, and unceasing care.
>
> O bring on in safety those for whom we pray,
> And prosper their journey with strength day by day,
> Till soon through Thy goodness we meet once again
> Together to praise Thee, the Lamb that was slain.
>
> These ten years of service alone for Thy sake,
> O Lord of the harvest, we pray Thee to take,
> Great praise, and great glory alone to Thy Name,
> Whose great loving kindness is always the same.
>
> O God of all mercy, continue to bless,
> The lone suffering lepers in all their distress,
> Thy grace is sufficient for all their deep need,
> Thy love all abounding, for such Thou did'st bleed.
>
> Good news for the leper, good news for the lost,
> Redemption is purchased, at so great a cost,
> Hallelujah ! for those who rejoicing can say
> On poor Robben Island, I am " happy " to-day.
>
> We welcome our brother and sister again
> And hail their return for His sake who was slain,
> Together expecting, and waiting the One
> Who's promised so surely, He quickly will come.
>
> E. A. M

GRANGETOWN.
   May 20th, 1899.

CHAPTER XI.

A VISIT TO PONDOLAND.

I had no intention when I commenced to bring into shape the foregoing extracts, to have said anything concerning my visit to Pondoland, but to have confined myself strictly to work amongst the lepers. However, in order that the book may become intelligible and more interesting to the reader, I have decided to insert therein a few items regarding the visit of my dear wife and myself, to that country.

For some years I had been able to read—imperfectly—the *Xosa* language, but knew very little of its foundation. Having an intense desire to understand it, I sought for a Kaffir teacher, and found one in Mr Mdelombo, whom I had met in Port Elizabeth a few years before. This minister undertook to teach me. And after a few months' instruction, he remarked to me one day that what I needed now was to get right in amongst the natives. About this time I read in the *Echoes of Service*, a letter from Mr W. Barton, who was then in charge of the Elim Mission Station, Pondoland East. The letter read thus : " I do not see my way clear to come home, unless I have some trustworthy person to take charge of the station , I cannot leave the work to a native."

I felt very much impressed by this letter, and putting the two things together, *i.e.* my teacher's

Mr Fred Elliot among the lepers

WORKERS IN NATAL AND PONDOLAND.
Back Row—Mr Fellingham, Miss Dunbar, Mr Oram, Miss Biffen.
Front Row—Mr and Mrs Madgwick and baby, Mr and Mrs Pugh and baby Gibbs, Mr and Mrs Gibbs.

A VISIT TO PONDOLAND

suggestion, and Mr Barton's letter, I at once wrote the latter for a few particulars regarding the healthiness of the country, etc., but holding out no promise to relieve him. In about six weeks' time, I received the following reply: "Climate perfect, no fevers. But, if you decide to come, you must not come alone; the loneliness is too intense, you must bring your wife."

Up to this time I had said nothing to my wife, but simply made it a matter of prayer. However, on reading Mr Barton's letter, she expressed her willingness to go, "if it be the Lord's will." So on the 25th of March 1903, we sailed from Cape Town for East London, where we were detained for a fortnight on account of the little boat, the *Umzumvubo*, undergoing repairs. We arrived at Port St John's on a Sunday afternoon, after a stormy voyage. There is a heavy sandbank at the entrance to the Port, and it was most interesting to watch the old captain, with coat off and sleeves turned up, navigating the boat over the bank. We were heartily glad to set foot once more on *terra firma*.

At 3 a.m. we were aroused and requested to take our seats in the post-cart for Lusikisiki, a distance of thirty-six miles. We can never forget our first impressions on ascending the road out of Port St John's. On either side of the Umzumvubo River, towering up into the sky, are the densely wooded mountains known as the "Gates of St John's." How sublime it all seemed. Oh, this great August, God! No wonder David cried out as he scanned the heavens; "What is man, that Thou art mindful of him, and the Son of Man that Thou visitest him" (Psa. viii.).

ROBBEN ISLAND

Two hours hard going, brought us to a place where we had to cross the Umzumvubo River, on a large pontoon, and we arrived at Lusikisiki about noon the same day, having changed our mules three times.

There we met Mr Barton for the first time. He responding to my " Praise the Lord ! " as we clasped each others hands, with " Hallelujah."

A journey of eight miles over open veldt, and we reached Elim Mission Station, towards the evening, and had the pleasure of meeting Mrs Barton also.

Mr Barton remained with us for five weeks before leaving for Scotland, so that he was able to initiate me into the work, and give me further help with the language.

I had already done a little riding, but here I had to learn how to handle a tricky little Pondo pony. One needs to possess something of the limpet nature to stick on their backs. I got my first experience of the Pondo pony after our second week in the country, when Mr Barton sent me on an errand about six or eight miles away, to a place I had never seen, the road to which I knew absolutely nothing of. You can readily imagine I was not very far on the road, or sheep track, before I found myself in a difficulty.

The natives put the usual questions, " Where had I come from, and where was I going ? " I told them where I had come from, but in telling them where I was going I used the wrong word, which I subsequently remembered meant "*going to earth*," and as far as my pony was concerned I might have gone to the earth again and again, and he would have made for home as quickly as his heels would have allowed

A VISIT TO PONDOLAND

him, leaving me to my fate, for he was a pony borrowed from a chief !

However, He who led Israel of old through a waste howling wilderness, had promised never to leave me, nor forsake me.

The Pondos are a very simple folk, and as Mr Barton remarked, " should be treated like a badly brought up lot of children." Whatever else the Pondo may lack, in the way of understanding, he is certainly not wanting in *patience*, and is capable of giving the missionary a good lesson in that respect. For instance, he will loiter about the Mission Station from sunrise to sunset for a pinch of salt, and if the Missionary deems it wise now and again to allow him to return to his kraal without his little luxury, then he lifts his hand, and with a pleasant smile on his face bids you adieu, only to pay you another visit the following morning, possibly before you have begun to rub your eyes ; and so he continues until patience has had its perfect work (not in him but in you), and subsequently he gets his well-earned bit of salt.

As far as I can judge, the Pondos are a quiet, inoffensive trible, not so warlike as the Zulus. In fact Mr Barton considers them great cowards, and that he could keep any number at bay with an old rifle.

In some respects, work among these people differs from that of the natives of Central Africa ; there they live in villages, but here in kraals or single huts ; thus, in order to reach them, a horse is indispensable for visiting the kraals. The natives come together on the Mission Station twice every week, Lord's Day being the principal gathering. Meetings were held throughout the day, finishing up about 5 p.m., so as to allow those from a distance to return before sunset. Those days were amongst the happiest of my Christian life—the unity and peace that prevailed was very blessed. True, we did not witness many conversions, for the Pondo has no intention whatever of believing your message. He thinks that by condescending to attend your Services, he has paid both you and your God a great compliment, and so returns to his kraal satisfied. Was there not a time when many of us were no better, with all our advantages? Did we not do practically the same thing? Shall we then blame the poor heathen in his darkness, or rather pity him?

A Gospel Service for Europeans was held in the Magistrate's Court-room, Lusikisiki, once a month. Messrs Robinson and Green, connected with the South African General Mission, came down from Umtata, and I usually went in from Elim. This Service was arranged when the moon was about full, to enable us to ride back to the Mission Station in the light of it. As a rule I reached home between eleven and twelve, my wife having been entirely alone on the Station. After a time, I felt convinced that it was not altogether right to leave her unprotected, and gave up going any longer. However, my visits were not without some little encouragement, for the Magistrate's clerk, Mr C. S. Eckardt, was led to accept Christ through a private conversation. I subsequently baptized him at Wynberg, and he was received into fellowship with believers there. He is still in Pondoland—Assistant Resident Magistrate.

A VISIT TO PONDOLAND

We provided a tea and reception meeting to welcome Mr and Mrs Barton on their return, when a goodly number of the natives, with two or three Chiefs, came together. The Pondos are very fond of them and were delighted to see them back.

Soon after their arrival, we returned to Wynberg, having been absent about sixteen months, and although our stay among the Pondos was so short, yet we found it difficult to break away from them. It is not easy to explain the fact that we are drawn very strongly towards these dear people—perhaps we ought to say with those who stood before Moses, confounded, " This is the finger of God."

CHAPTER XII.

BACK TO ROBBEN ISLAND.

17th August 1904.—My brother and I went over to the Island to-day, my first visit since our return from Pondoland. My brother faithfully continued in the work during my absence. It has been a heart-melting time for me; dear Lm. is almost blind, but quiet and peaceful. We found young J. M. also calm and confident, confined to bed, and much changed in appearance since I last saw him. He is very happy in the Lord, and it is blessed to hear him speak of Jesus. I look upon him as *the* bright shining light on the Island to-day.

Poor B., who formerly lived such an ungodly life, is also very happy—he is a striking trophy of grace.

1st September.—Joseph and I were among the lepers again; we had the joy and privilege of speaking to a good many. Young J. M. was a little better. As soon as we entered his room he said: "Oh, Mr Fish, I am glad that I am a child of God." We found the man to whom we spoke a fortnight ago, happy in knowing his sins forgiven; thus the word of encouragement comes to our hearts, "And let us not be weary in well-doing, for in due season we shall reap, if we faint not" (Gal. vi. 9).

16th September.—We have been much helped of the Lord in visiting the patients to-day. Dear young

BACK TO ROBBEN ISLAND

M. is still bright, and there are evidences of God working with a few others.

23rd September.—Was alone on the Island to-day. My heart was deeply touched as I noticed a few nice young girls in one of the European Wards, looking so sad, and in tears regarding their sorrowful condition. I met a patient to-day, English born; this is the first that we have met; he told me that there were also two others there, who were brought over quite recently.

28th September. — Joseph and I were over, and spoke to a goodly number. We enjoyed a talk with some little girls, but Oh, the time is far too limited to deal with many eager faces on all sides—one might hear them say, "Aren't you coming to me?" We were told of a man on the Island to-day, who has been deaf and dumb from a little child, but is now able to hear and speak.

14th October.—There was an unpleasant swell on this morning, and by some means or other, I felt a little discouraged, having left home with a severe headache. The adversary tried to persuade me to give up the Island work now. Thus the arch-enemy is always on the alert, and ready to take every advantage he can, of our physical weakness.

However, the Lord knew how to encourage my faith, by giving me a specially nice time with the patients, and Satan, I trust, has again been defeated.

I am dealing with a young girl in No. 10, who, I trust, is not far from the Kingdom. She is about seventeen years of age, and of English parents.

21st October.—To-day, my brother and I visited

ROBBEN ISLAND

both male and female locations. Had a further conversation with the young girl in No. 10, but she has not yet found peace.

3rd November.—Had a very precious time among the patients to-day; the young girl, Maggie, to whom we spoke last week, is not yet saved. I had a few words with some Kaffirs, one of whom was visibly affected.

7th November.—I did not intend going to the Island this morning, but whilst taking my breakfast, I felt a strong conviction that I ought to go, so I went. (This is not an uncommon experience of mine.) And I have reason to believe that the Lord has blessed His Word to one young woman. Oh, to know something more of the experiences of the perfect Servant, " He wakeneth morning by morning, He wakeneth mine ear to hear as the learner " (Isa. l. 4, R.V.).

18th November.—Joseph and I were kept busy dealing with precious souls, for whom there is practically no hope for the healing of the body. Thank God, we have the healing balm for the soul. I believe the young girl spoken to the previous week, was helped a little further to-day, but I cannot say that she has yet accepted Christ. Oh, how little one can do among over six hundred poor lepers, scattered over the island, with the few hours at our disposal.

27th November.—I was alone on the Island to-day. The weather was very unpleasant; we had to steam half-speed, and nearly came into collision with a large sailing ship. We brought back eighteen lunatics from the Island to-day.

16th December.—Poor old B. has been greatly

BACK TO ROBBEN ISLAND

cheered by a visit from his wife, whom he had not seen for several years. On my return this evening, I heard of the serious illness of my brother's little girl, an only child.

17*th December.*—The news came this morning that Joseph's little daughter has died. This is sad indeed, and we deeply sympathise with them in their great sorrow.

13*th January* 1905.—My brother, Miss Prentice, of Central Africa, and I were over to-day. We had an interesting time with the patients. The passage to the Island was by no means pleasant, deeply loaded with 110 passengers, and a strong south-east wind; far too many people for such a small boat; I fear we shall come to grief some day.

18th *January.*—I was over alone, and felt deeply grateful to God, for such a golden opportunity to tell these poor lepers of a Saviour, mighty and willing to save. Had a nice word with Vera K.; I do trust that she may soon be able to lay hold on Christ.

June.—I have made many visits to the Island since the above date, but have taken no note of them.

2*nd June.*—My brother and I were over again. Opportunities to testify for the Lord abound, our only regret is that our time is so limited.

14*th June.*—We were over on Wednesday this week, and had a real good time with the patients. They are always so willing and ready to listen to anything we have to tell them from the Word of God. We remained among the male patients, but each of us going in different direction to make the best use of our time. I soon found myself behind some old huts, amidst swarms of flies, telling out the story of redeeming love, to about a half-dozen of eager listeners. Later, I found myself in one of the Wards, with a number of poor leper boys around me : Blessed privilege !

30*th June*.—I found Mr Lm. rather weak. He does not think that he will be here much longer, and longs to see his wife. He says " I had once what I thought was joy, but I have had more real joy during these few years that I have known the Lord, on Robben Island, than during the whole of the fifty years of my life before. ' The will of the Lord be done.' I know, nay, I am sure, when God calls me, I shall go to be with Christ, where neither pain, sickness, nor suffering can ever come." Poor Mr Ls. told me to-day that they have turned his children away from the Seminary on account of leprosy being in the family. This is the sorest affliction these poor people can have. Oh ! the stigma of this horrible disease ! His first wife was an inmate of the Robben Island Institute for four and a half years. She fell asleep six years ago. He afterwards married again. His second wife only lived eleven months. And shortly after the death of his second wife, he himself was brought to Robben Island a leper, where he lived but a few years, and died, being sorely afflicted. I saw him the day before he died, and read to him, 1 Peter, chap i.

28*th July*.—Joseph and I were over to-day. I was grieved and disappointed to find that the girl Maggie, of whom I had great hopes, now turns out to be a Roman Catholic at heart ; however, I feel I must do as David did, " encourage my heart in the Lord."

BACK TO ROBBEN ISLAND

4th August.—It was unpleasant weather, but we had a refreshing time on the Island. We called to see a man who was very ill, in a separate room, De R. by name. After speaking to him for some time we discovered that he was one who some while previous, when Joseph was dealing with him about his soul, suddenly caught hold of my brother saying, "I will shake your life out of you." Now we found him saved through the blood of the Cross, and humbled to the dust. How wonderful are God's ways! He who could tame the maniac of Mark v. could also subdue this poor leper too, "leaving him sitting, clothed, and in his right mind."

18th August.—Mrs P. has been dying for the past three weeks; she is very low, but happy in the Lord. Her disease is of such a nature, that it is well nigh impossible to approach close to her bed. But she is only one of many on that island of misery and sorrow. Eight fresh cases were taken over to-day, amongst them being a Mrs B., from B——. She wept bitterly saying that "she could easier suffer her bodily affliction, if it was ten times worse, than endure the separation from her husband and family." Sorrow! Sorrow!! Nothing but sorrow there.

25th August 1905.—Joseph went to Murray's Bay, whilst I remained with the men, and had a good time with a few natives. In speaking to B., I learned that some plain words spoken to him about five weeks back, led to a definite acceptance of Christ, and now he is rejoicing in the knowledge of sins forgiven. He told me that he went to the Lord after he was spoken to, and said: "Lord, if I am wrong

ROBBEN ISLAND

show it to me. Let me see my true condition "; "and the Lord revealed it to me." This was refreshing news to my soul.

13th October.—Two cases were added to the number to-day, one a little boy, Lucas, from Wynberg.

We heard that a fine young fellow who has been assisting the doctor in post-mortem work, had by some means contracted the disease. He came across to Cape Town several times for examination, and finally it was decided that he was a leper. He knew that he would be segregated, and rather than face the terrible future, he returned to the Island that evening, drank poison, and died. Oh, the tragedy of this awful affliction!

31st August 1906.—I felt specially constrained to go over to-day, and have reason to believe that the Word was blessed to one man. He simply rained down tears as I spoke to him of God's love. It is marvellous how these people can weep. One can readily understand Luke vii. 38, after seeing a poor leper weep. "Began to wash His feet with tears." —"Rain tears on His feet."

14th September.—Whilst in No. 1 Ward, I was requested to see a man who had been placed in a small room outside, the smell from his poor body being so bad, that he could not be kept in the large ward. His feet were simply rotting off, and it was difficult to go sufficiently near to speak to him. I believe he was left trusting in Christ, and died a few days after.

26th September.—An interesting time with both men and women. I am not able to say much in

BACK TO ROBBEN ISLAND

Kaffir, but am thankful for the little that I can manage, as it is the royal road to their hearts.

On our return the boat broke down, but fortunately another was steaming into the harbour and took us in tow.

5th October.—Joseph and I were in Jas. M.'s room, his mother also being present. We had a solemn time with him touching his spiritual life, as he has become cold of late ; others get him to play the piano at their birthday parties. Whilst on our knees we sang " When I survey the wondrous Cross, on which the Prince of Glory died." His heart was touched, and I hope it will be the turning point. How we need to understand the word of Peter : " Kept by the power of God, through faith." It is mine to trust, but His to keep.

12th October.—To-day we were on the Island again. My brother went down to the females—he often does—and thus we are able to cover more ground. I remained with the men all day, and was helped in speaking to a few natives again to-day. Had a nice time also with some lads, who were visibly affected. May it please God to touch their hearts, whilst they are young and tender.

19th October.—Thank God for the opportunity of seeing the patients once more. There are heart-rending scenes on that Island. It is there, one understands a little of what " the groaning creation " means ; no words of mine could convey what a personal visit to that Island would.

26th October.—Mr and Mrs M. were over, so I did not call to see their son Jas. I met with an in-

ROBBEN ISLAND

teresting case in No. 1. A young man who was confined to bed, sobbed aloud as I spoke to him of Christ; tracing Him from the point of betrayal to Pilate's judgement hall, thence to Calvary. Poor fellow; with tears he assured me that he was resting alone upon the finished work of Christ. Oh, how we need to preach Him, His Words were, " And I, if I be lifted up from the earth, will draw all men unto me " (John xii. 32). Mr Ls. is evidently breaking up.

31st October.—Met Mrs Lm. on the boat this morning; she had received a message to say that her husband was very weak. I just touched at his room on my way to the wards, and found him very weak, but calm and peaceful. I found Mr Lb. also in bed, face terribly swollen. I spoke solemnly to him about his soul; he was deeply grateful for all I said to him.

7th November.—Been to the Island again to-day. Found Mr Lm. a little better; his wife has returned to the mainland. I had an earnest time with Mr Lb., but he is still in the region of darkness. Many others were spoken to. I am thankful for another day among the poor lepers. It was very unpleasant on the water, some got wet.

16th November.—My brother and I were over again, and had a good day amongst the patients: it was refreshing to my own soul, whilst speaking to a few believers on the coming of the Lord.

19th November.—I was at Robben Island to-day, accompanied by Mr J. Wright, who went over on business for his firm. I was able to pass him through some of the wards on my Government Permit. Mr Lm. seems brighter to-day. He says he is patiently

BACK TO ROBBEN ISLAND

waiting to enter the pearly gate, and felt a little disappointed in not being taken Home in his recent illness. In speaking to him about some of the vanities of this world, he remarked, " The world could not satisfy, Christ alone can do that; Oh," said he, " that I could tell the world so; I would shout it out, every hour, night and day. What would I not give to stand in the City Hall, to-night, before 10,000 people; I would shout it out with all my might— ' Christ alone can satisfy.' Tell it out my brother; shout aloud, that nothing but Christ can satisfy. Tell them a poor leper on Robben Island, says so." My heart was stirred as I saw the earnestness of this poor blind leper. The Lord gave me a very blessed day, and I am sure that several were helped.

16th January 1907.—In course of conversation with brother Lm., he reminded me of a Malay patient who died on the Island a few years ago, confessing Christ as his Saviour. The Malay had said that he thanked God that men had come to the Island, and told him of Jesus. He believed that Jesus was the Son of God, and the only way to be saved was through His death, and that he had accepted Him as his Saviour, though he would submit to the rites of the Malay burial. " Yet," he said, " I am not a Malay inwardly." This is extraordinary ! for you will rarely find a Malay to admit that Christ was the Son of God. I had a word with a poor old man just brought to the Island, at eighty-one years of age, and in an advanced stage of the disease, but I got very little response from him. Few are brought to Christ at that age.

25th January.—Was kept busy on the Island.

ROBBEN ISLAND

Called at Mr L'.s room, and met two of his sons there; had a real good time with them about their souls; subsequently found one of them trusting in the Lord. A wound received in the leg during the Boer War, was the means of leading him to Christ. The other showed no interest in spiritual things. One was a doctor, and before his father was brought to the Island, he persuaded him to eat fine gravel, believing that it would cure the leprosy. The poor father did so for a time, but all in vain!

7th February.—I met a young man, recently come from Port Elizabeth. I questioned him as to how he had contracted the disease. He said that some one had told him that it was from eating badly cured fish. I told him that I had not much confidence in that theory. I asked him how long he had had it. He told me that it was just at the close of the Boer War. After hearing his story I was convinced as to the way he had contracted it.

At the close of a little Service to-day (for women), two came to me expressing their gratitude for what they had heard. One was stone blind, and minus hands and feet! I was told not to forget them, but to come again, as they loved to listen to God's Word.

21st February.—Had a further talk with the young man from Port Elizabeth; he appeared to be interested in the Word, and I hope ere long he will be brought to Christ.

12th April.—My brother and I had a good time with the patients.

22nd April.—Miss R. Cane and Miss Smith went over. We were able to deal with a fair number about

ASSEMBLY AT MANSFIELD, NATAL.

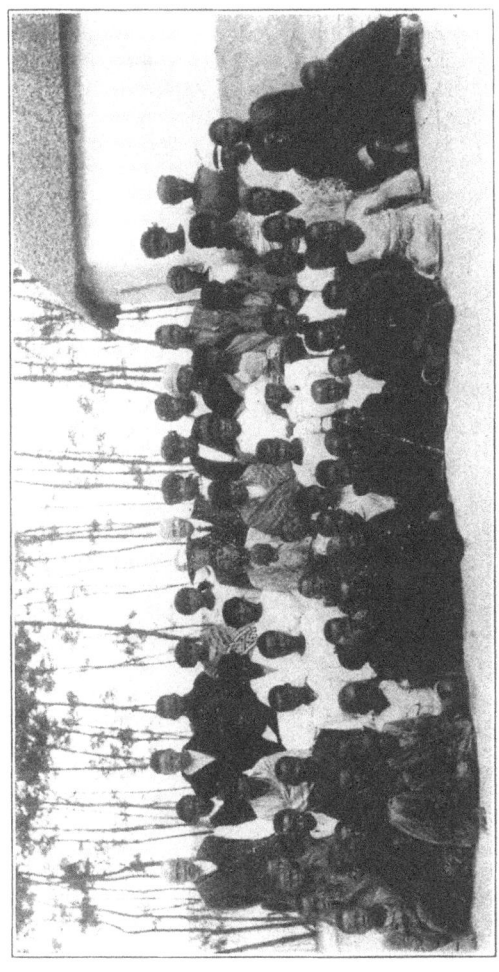

Mr and Mrs Sharp (who were on a visit) are in the centre, and old Jacob, the Evangelist, is on the extreme left, while in front are some Sunday School scholars.

CONFERENCE GROUP, KALEBA.

Back Row—Miss Elliot, Mrs Higgins, Mrs Turner (L.M.S.), Mrs Anton.
Second Row—Mr Crawford, Mrs W. Lammond, Mrs G. W. Sims, Mrs Crawford (with Gwen Sims), Mr Anton.
Third Row—Mr M'Kenzie, Mr W. Lammond, Mrs Last.
Front Row—Mr Ellis, Tommy Higgins, Mr G. W. Sims, Mr Last.

their souls, as well as imparting words of cheer to a few of His own children.

3rd May—Brothers Besford and Hamilton were with me, and were interested in what they saw. A lad in No. 1 Ward was in a sad condition, evidently nearing his end. After a talk with him, he assured me that he was trusting in the Saviour.

Mr le Roux was buried, and we stood for a while during the funeral service, which was very impressive. Then we went on to the females. Whilst in one of the wards, I heard the voice of poor Mrs Little, and on looking through the bars of the window near to where I was sitting, I saw her in a small enclosure, crawling about upon her hands and knees with her face turned rigidly upwards, and mouth open wide, making a moaning noise. I called her by name, and she at once recognised my voice, " Where are you Mr Fish ? " I replied, " By the window." " Let me feel you." I said I will put my hand upon your arm. No sooner had I done so than she clasped my hand in both of hers. I must confess that for the moment I felt a little uneasy, and could only entreat her to loose it, which I am thankful to say she did after a moment or two. She is a dear child of God, but now deranged in mind. Oh, for a more grateful heart to God, for His mercies to me ! Ten more patients were taken over to-day.

15th May.—The lad to whom I spoke last week died, soon after I had left him.

7th June.—Had a precious time as usual. How important it is to be led to the right individuals at the proper time. God's service then becomes a delight.

ROBBEN ISLAND

14th June.—Joseph was with me to-day and we had a nice talk with Jas. M., who is much subdued in spirit. We trust the Lord will bless the Word to his soul, and he may " soon recover himself out of the snare of the devil." We had a precious time also with two women, and I feel sure they were helped.

5th July.—My soul was much refreshed in speaking to some of the patients, especially to one believer, who surprised me when I saw how clearly he apprehended the truth of the Lord's Coming. I had an interesting time also with a Roman Catholic. He was prepared to hear anything from the Word of God, and assured me after a lengthy conversation, that he was trusting in the Saviour.

19th July.—The young man to whom I spoke a fortnight ago, and who was so ill, is now screened off. I tried to come near to speak to him, but it was impossible. How can one sufficiently thank God, for preservation from this loathsome disease?

16th July.—Another day amongst the lepers. Whatever there may be of discouragement in labouring on Robben Island, there is that which more than makes up for it, namely, the readiness on the part of the patients to listen to the Word, which unquestionably is doing its own steady work : " He that believeth shall not make haste."

CHAPTER XIII.

TROPHIES OF GRACE AMONG THE LEPERS.

17th January 1908.—Have been laid aside for the past two months.

Joseph and I were over again; we were sorry to find dear Lm. very weak, evidently nearing his end. We had a very nice talk with him, and could only praise God for the grace given him to patiently submit to His will.

28th January.—My brother is over alone, as I am confined to bed. I deeply regret not being able to go to the Island to-day, as dear Lm. was buried, having died the day before.

This is another trophy of Grace, and an object of suffering loosed from earth, to join the ransomed above.

During the fourteen years that he was confined to Robben Island as a leper, his life was a witness to the saving and keeping power of the Gospel. He looked forward to being with the Lord, with much confidence and joy.

21st August.—For several months past, I have not been able to visit the lepers, on account of illness. But I am happy to say, that I am so far recovered as to continue the weekly visits with my brother. It has been a very great joy to my heart, to see the

ROBBEN ISLAND

patients once more, and to testify to the goodness of God in a special manner. He has given evidence of His saving power in a few cases, and we have been enabled to cheer the hearts of some of His poor weary children. The truth concerning the Lord's return has been quite a fresh revelation to them, they having never been taught anything but a general resurrection.

We were on the Island two days last week; Mr Isseneger was with us one day, and was deeply touched by the sights.

Dr Wilson Smith, of Bath, went over with us to-day, and was much interested in going through some of the wards with Dr Moon, who explained several of the worst cases to him.

Poor B. still lingers on, a most pitiable object for human eyes to behold, yet he is bright with the hope of soon being released from his misery, to be for ever with the Lord.

A very dear Kaffir, Seppe Jack, told me of his conversion recently. It was very touching. He was shut up for eight days' examination, during which time he was much broken and wept a good deal. And it was, he says, there, that God convinced him that he was a lost sinner. He found much comfort from the words of a hymn, in Kaffir. We turned up the hymn and sang it. Poor fellow, the tears rolled down his cheeks as we sang. I believe he is sincerly trusting in the Lord.

In passing through the wards last week, I came across a man very ill in bed—a *very* bad case. The effluvium from his body was absolutely unbearable

TROPHIES OF GRACE AMONG THE LEPERS

and it was as much as I could do, to remain with him five minutes. What an object of absolute pity he is! I asked him what he was resting on for eternity; he replied, "On nothing in myself, sir, but wholly on the finished work of Christ." Rarely does one get such a satisfactory answer, and with such a true ring.

14th July 1909.—It is now close on a year since I made any notes of my visits to the Island. One reason is, that I have not been going over as regularly as I used to do. For I find that the strong south-east gales affect my head very seriously. And I am often hindered in my service for the Lord on the mainland. However, I make a point of going over when the weather is favourable.

Was over to-day. Among others, I met with a man who was really anxious to be helped. I pointed out to him the necessity of the *new birth*, at which he expressed his utter astonishment. Oh, the terrible ignorance among these poor creatures!

Enjoyed a word with about a dozen boys in No. 5 Ward. Poor B., died about two months ago, after fifteen years' confinement on the Island. I have no doubt that he is at home with the Lord. Poor fellow, he was a most pitiable sight; blind, with neither hands nor feet, and covered with open ulcers. Poor young J. M. died somewhere in about the beginning of the year—rather suddenly—after being on the Island six years. I was very much disappointed in that young man towards the last. He was only nineteen years of age, when he was stricken down with that terrible disease, and brought to Robben Island, where, under rather peculiar circumstances he was brought to the Lord, and for a time he became very bright.

He was brought to the Lord in the following way. I missed the boat one day and consequently was left on the Island for two days. After cabling to my wife, I settled down to the inevitable. In the evening I returned to the wards, where I met, in a private room, the above-mentioned young man for the first time. It was a room occupied by two young men, lepers, and brothers in the flesh. It was suggested that we should read something from the Word of God, and also sing a few hymns. There and then, unknown to me for the moment, God spoke to him. I rose to leave, but he followed me outside, and then told me that God had spoken to him. He said, " I could not let you go without first telling you that God has blessed His Word to my soul, and I have here and now accepted Christ as my Saviour." He became very bright, but his aptness in playing the piano, became a snare to him. However, I have no question about his being with the Lord. How wonderful are God's ways! I was stranded on the Island, so that I might lead that young man to Christ.

26*th July*.—Was over again to-day—not very pleasant weather. Met with several interesting cases; but, Oh, one has to speak to these poor creatures in the most simple manner, and even then, in some cases, it means months, yea, years, before they are able with any clearness to apprehend the truth. One dear fellow, was simply enraptured with the truth of our Lord's coming!

TROPHIES OF GRACE AMONG THE LEPERS

2nd May 1910.—I felt encouraged by a conversation with an Englishman who was all through the Boer War, at the close of which he developed leprosy, and was brought to the Island, where he has been for seven years. I often tried to speak to him about his soul, but he would never listen; his heart was like adamant against the Word of God.

On Monday last, the Lord spoke to him in a wonderful manner, and as I afterwards reflected, I could only praise God for the wisdom and tact He gave me in dealing with him. What supreme power there is in the Word of God. It is clearly not by wisdom of man's words, the hardest hearts are sometimes reached on the simplest lines. The result was, however, that he promised me definitely to read the Bible, which he is not altogether ignorant of, and asked me to come and see him again, such as he had never done before.

23rd January 1911.—I am thankful for the privilege allowed me of visiting the patients once more, and to tell them of a God of compassion and love, " not willing that any should perish, but that all should come to repentance." And that is salvation, even for a leper. There are on the Island at the present time 583 patients, but this is by no means all the lepers in South Africa. There are other large Institutes in the country, and also about 2000 still at large. What an awful scourge this is upon our beautiful sunny Africa !

I am afraid that under the present system of dealing with these unfortunate creatures, the disease will spread more and more. For instance a woman comes to see her husband, perhaps with three or four children. She first goes round to most of the patients

ROBBEN ISLAND

in the ward and shakes hands—if perchance there be a hand to shake. She then goes to her husband, and in addition to shaking his hand, plants a few kisses on his poor leprous face. Then she sits down and takes out her bounties, fruit, etc. After spending the day in this manner, she again greets all in the ward, and returns to the mainland. The first friend she meets is greeted with a shake of the hand. It is obvious that such a practice can only endanger the public, and help to spread the affliction. Doctors admit that " segregation on Robben Island is only a half-hearted thing."

1st February.—I took over a number of Dutch almanacs to-day, which the patients were glad to receive. It was difficult to break away, so kept at it until three o'clock.

There are four doctors resident on the island now, one of whom is an expert, and gives the whole of his time to research work. After all, how entirely beyond the most brainy men is this disease! Even the doctors themselves differ in their opinions, some saying it is contagious, others that it is not. There are some facts about leprosy which make it most puzzling. It has been known that a child of leprous parents grew up, married, and showed no sign of the disease. " The leprous microbe," says Dr Sandes, " cannot live in the light; as soon as it comes into the light it dies, and yet, whilst it remains in the system, no organic has yet been found to destroy it, without breaking the tissues of the body and killing the patient." How hopeless then is this terrible malady! We understand that consumptive microbes float in the air, and are communicable, but this is not the case with leprosy. Warm blood has been taken from the sufferer and immediately injected into some animal, viz., a cat or dog, but no ill effects have followed. This malignant disease seems to prefer the nose for its stronghold, and the result is, that that member becomes flat, and often broken. It is said that in some cases, the disease dries up after a number of years, and for the time being, the patient is no source of danger to anyone.

6th February.—I was greatly cheered to-day on hearing of the last moments of Miss R. I think my brother was a great help to her. Realising that her end was near, she sent for Mr Lo., to whom she had been engaged for some years. She told him that she knew that her time to depart this life was near, and that she was quite confident she was going to be with the Lord. She urged him to think seriously of the matter for himself. Then followed a request to those gathered around, " Sing, ' Rock of Ages cleft for me.' " As they sang the closing verse, she breathed her last. This has made a deep impression on Mr Lo.

It turns out now, that when Mr Br. left his old quarters he left behind a number of Gospel tracts, amongst them being *God's way Salvation,* in Dutch, a book which I translated years ago. This very copy which had been used to the conversion of Mr Br., also became the means used to bring Lo. to the Lord. It appears that Lo. and another patient went to Br.'s old room, and among the waste paper found this book. Lo. is stone blind, but the other read it to him, and he was immediately impressed, so much

ROBBEN ISLAND

so that he requested his companion to bring the book away with him, and to explain it more fully, which he did with the above result. "Why," said he, "can a person not be saved, when it is so simple?" I called at Br.'s room, where I found Lo., who was quite willing to listen as never before, and as far as one can discern he is now trusting in Christ.

It is clear to me that the result of all these years of toil on Robben Island is, that a good foundation has been laid, so that whoever may be privileged to continue the work when we are no longer able, will find things comparatively easy, and doubtless will be allowed to reap more largely of our labours. So it will be; "one soweth and another reapeth, that both he that soweth, and he that reapeth may rejoice together" (John iv. 36).

15th February.—Glad to be able to visit the dear lepers again. Amongst those spoken to to-day, was a man who has been on the Island for twenty years, and who has also known the Lord for many years. A native sitting near us, as I repeated a hymn to him in Kaffir, exclaimed; "Oh, it's a blessed thing, sir, that you are able to help us, both in Dutch and Kaffir."

I saw the boys and girls in their new quarters to-day; one's heart is made sad as one looks at these young people, hopelessly afflicted, sent to that Island to linger out their days in misery.

28th February.—Three weeks ago I met a new arrival on the island, a young Jew, brought up and well educated in Cape Town. The story regarding this young man is sad in the extreme. It appears that about two years ago, he became alarmed with the condition of his hands, and knowing something of leprosy, he feared lest he might in some way have contracted it. He decided to first make known his fears to one or two of his fellow-students who were studying for doctors. Alas! his fears were not without foundation. His friends advised him to go to Germany and England at once, and consult the most eminent doctors. Consequently he took his departure almost immediately. That was in May 1910. After going to Germany, he crossed to England and entered a London hospital, where he was kept as a leper patient for four months. During his confinement, King George and Queen Mary visited the hospital and spoke to him, expressing their deep sympathy with him. In due course he was discharged, *incurable*, and had to face the inevitable, *i.e.* return to South Africa and be segregated on Robben Island, to there live and die a leper.

What all this means to a brain so intensely active as his is, none save He who reads the thoughts and intents of the heart, can fully know. I have had a most solemn word with him regarding his soul, and he has listened very attentively. Before I left him he expressed his deep appreciation for the interest I was taking in him, and assured me that he would be glad to see me at any time.

7th April.—I have been able to deal with several unsaved ones, some as dark as midnight concerning spiritual things. I met one poor old man, who has only been twelve days on the Island. He did not know whether he believed in Jesus or no. I asked if he knew he had had his breakfast. "Oh, yes,"

ROBBEN ISLAND

he said, " I am sure of that." How such cases cast one upon God ! H., a patient, has three sons there. Two are decided lepers ; a third has been employed as an attendant, for the past five years, and now they have grave fears that he has contracted the disease. I saw him to-day, and he certainly shows signs of it in his face. What a mysterious disease this is; it baffles the best of men.

19th April.—Messrs Crowhurst and le Riche were with me to-day, and as all of us are acquainted with the Dutch language, we were able to deal with a good number. We visited the huts at the back of the wards, where, I often say, we see the work proper. Our attention was drawn to one hut in particular, where a Kaffir woman, sitting on the bare ground (to say nothing of the filth), was preparing a duck for the saucepan. Of all the sights I ever saw, that certainly was the most sickening. As I looked at that poor soul with her awful leprous hands dealing with that dainty dish, presently to be enjoyed by herself and others, I said to myself, " Why are you not sitting there, a poor hopelessly afflicted leper like that woman ? " I could only answer—

> " Grace, Grace, all to Grace I owe ;
> Sin had left a crimson stain,
> He washed it white as snow."

The father of Heins has sued the Government for £1000 damages for detaining his son on the island as a leper. He was brought to the mainland to-day to be examined.

24th April.—Brother Furniss, from the Argentine,

TROPHIES OF GRACE AMONG THE LEPERS

went with me to-day. I could only show him a little of the work, with the limited time we have on the Island. Still what he saw impressed him very much, and I am sure he will not soon forget his visit We had a, solemn talk with the Jew. In the case of Heins, judgment has been given in favour of the defendant: the doctors having decided that he is a leper. Here now comes the difficulty; did he contract the disease, or was he predisposed to it?

8th May.—Poor Mr Ls. is becoming very weak; I think his end is near; he suffers a good deal, which is not usual in the majority of cases. He is, however, peaceful and calm. I read to him 1 Peter i., pointing out to him the unspeakable comfort there is to be found in the unchanging Word of God. I met a patient to-day, who with some others was transferred to Bloemfontein a year ago, but he was not at all satisfied, and requested the Government to allow him to return to the Island again. He says: " On the Island he gets something for his soul, but in Bloemfontein he gets nothing." He is a sincere believer, and I well remember the circumstances of his conversion.

19th January 1912.—I have made many visits since the above date, and had some most interesting times, but have taken no notes. Poor Mr Ls. has gone to be with the Lord; happy release for him. A little while back I called at No. 10 Ward, and saw Wiblin, but he was in a very sore way, and refused to listen to anything I had to say about the Lord. He said that he had been eight years on that Island, and had *done nothing else but curse God the whole of the time.*

ROBBEN ISLAND

And if I spoke to him about religion, he would curse me too. (This poor man has made me weep more than once. Oh, God keep my heart tender towards those poor outcasts.) I told him that his cursing would do him no good, and would do me no harm. However, he would not listen, and soon began to curse me, so I was obliged to leave him! Brother M'Bride, from Johannesburg, was with me to-day. We had a very happy day, and I was very much impressed with the tact our brother used in dealing with souls. On our rounds we called on Wiblin. I had said nothing to Mr M'Bride regarding this man, so that he was perfectly free to deal with him. Mr M'Bride spoke most tenderly to him; still he refused to listen, and soon began using bad language, so that we were again obliged to leave him.

But the other side of life was seen in a young woman, only three months on the island. We spoke to her of God's wondrous love, and told her what peace and joy could be hers now by trusting in Jesus. As we spoke to her of Christ dying on the Cross, the tears rolled down her cheeks; it was very touching, as I have often remarked, to see a poor leper weeping. She assured us before leaving, that she was trusting in the Saviour. We saw one poor fellow dying in No. 1, almost too awfully afflicted to approach.

22nd January.—Was over to-day. The man dying in No. 1 last week was now gone; I spoke to a few of the other patients, but one young man was in a most wretched condition bodily; I could only stay with him a few moments. How shall I describe his face? It is beyond words! Flesh all eaten away, nose gone, eyes eaten entirely out, and mouth beyond description! As one looks at such cases one is led to ask the question, " Was it for such the Son of God died the cruel death of the Cross ? " Then comes the grand old verse ; " God so loved the world." Oh, that cruel disease! Leprosy! Leprosy! Art thou a type of sin ?

31st January.—The dear patients were overjoyed in seeing us to-day ; some rushed into the ward as they heard our voices. This is very cheering.

Since the above date I have visited the Island on an average once a week, but have kept no regular account.

15th July.—Some few months back, a very respectable old man was brought to the island a leper. Strange to say he brought his coffin with him! It turns out that a few years ago he discovered an old cemetery dating back to the 16th Century. He started to work and soon got the whole thing renovated ; the old graves, which were overgrown, were again cleared, and now he wants to be buried among some of the old Dutch veterans. I believe he has obtained the consent of the Government to have his corpse taken from the island, and buried in the above cemetery, providing the coffin is lined inside with lead. I am glad to find that the dear old man knows the Lord. However, he may never require his lead coffin. It may be " the sky not the grave for his goal."

In February last, a lady and gentleman from Johannesburg went over with me. After going through some of the wards, I took them to the top of the Island, where they could see the work proper.

ROBBEN ISLAND

Oh, the privilege of entering one of those little huts occupied by two or three poor lepers, and in the most simple manner possible pointing them to the finished work of Christ. Angels might envy our privilege! Oh, the joy of being allowed to lead one poor leper to the Lord! It is a foretaste of heaven below. I said to my friends, "Tell me, is it possible for one person to do anything like justice to the work in so little time on the Island?" They replied, "Six persons would not be too many for the work." I took them to see poor Wiblin, but his attitude was unchanged; he only swears at me if I speak to him of the Lord.

Mr Henry Hynd, and his daughter Flora, went over with me one day, and like most who visit the lepers for the first time, were deeply moved by the misery on that Island. We called on Sergt. W. Mr Hynd had a nice word with him. A young coloured brother (Brummer) went over one day. We got the patients together and had little Services here and there; they were greatly pleased by the earnestness of this young brother, who speaks freely in Dutch.

Last week I was over twice, and had the pleasure of dear brother F. S. Arnot's company. This was his first visit to the lepers. We had a profitable time as we moved quietly round among the patients.

Yesterday Mr Stein went over with me. (He is from India.) We visited several of the wards and he was touched very much as he saw the misery and suffering. He said he would consider it a kindness if the doctor shortened the life of some. But that, of course, is altogether out of the question.

TROPHIES OF GRACE AMONG THE LEPERS

11*th October*.—My brother has been in England for the past year, and for the last three weeks I have been holding special services at Stickland, a short distance up the main line. However, my brother has returned from England, and we were both on the Island to-day. Poor Greyling was overwhelmed with joy at seeing us again. My brother had a word with Wiblin to-day, but as far as we can see, his attitude is unchanged.

16*th October*.—I was over alone, and kept very busy all day. Met with one very interesting case among the coloured lepers, quite above the average for intelligence.

Poor Greyling is very weak. He is longing for a little spring water from the mainland ; I hope to send him some. He quoted the words of David, when he had escaped to the cave of Adullam, " Oh, that one would give me drink of the water of the well of Bethlehem." Thank God, he has drunk of the living water, and it makes him long for more, not so much of the earthly springs, but of the heavenly. Another, who is David's Lord cried, " I thirst," but no mighty men were found to fetch Him a drop of water, otherwise how should Psa. xxii. 15, and lxix. 21 be fulfilled ?

18*th October*.—On my arrival at the Island this morning I learned that poor Greyling had passed away on the Sunday evening, so that there was no need for the water. He fell asleep very peacefully, and was conscious up to the last. " Mark the perfect man, behold the upright, for the end of that man is peace " (Psa. xxxvii. 37).

ROBBEN ISLAND

11th November.—Mrs W. Southall was with me to-day ; we were kept busy visiting the different wards, but oh, the needs are simply appalling. Think for a moment of 620 helpless people, scattered over the Island; sometimes one is not able to reach more than a dozen in a day, *i.e.*, to deal with each thoroughly. We were impressed while listening to the story of one dear coloured woman, who has been already twenty-one years on the Island ; she had been a slave under the Portuguese Government, and was brought down from the Zambesi. As a little girl she remembered seeing Dr Livingstone. It was a joy to find that she is trusting in the Lord. Oh, what a history ! From slavery, to a leper on Robben Island ! Thank God, she has been emancipated from a yet greater slavery—from the bondage of sin. Her skin is as black as ebony, no hands, no feet, yet happy in the Lord. My heart truly rejoiced as I thought of the crowning act to such a sad life, when she with all the redeemed will shine out in the beauty and glory of the Lord. Then will the truth of Luke xiii. 29, be realised in the highest degree possible.

April 1913.—Looking backward over the past few months, one feels grateful to God for the privilege given to visit these poor lepers, and speak to them face to face. To tell them of God's great love, and point them in simple, plain, everyday language, to the Lamb of God, who taketh away the sin of the world ; and then to witness what joy and comfort it imparts, one is more than repaid for any self-sacrifice made. There are difficulties in connection with the work, due chiefly to their early training, and we find it by no means easy to disabuse their minds of those first impressions.

I found a few very nice Christians among the Kaffirs. They are anxious that I should have a reading of the Scriptures with them every time I go over; I am not able to do much in the Kaffir language, but another difficulty is the lack of time. Hence I have often longed for the time, when I may be allowed to live on the Island, at least for a year, or so. Generally speaking, there is more firmness of character among the natives than among the coloured people, though, I must candidly admit that one does find now and again some real gems among the coloured folk. I might say, in addition to the privilege of carrying the Gospel to these poor creatures, we have been enabled to minister to them largely in temporal things, especially in fruit. This has been done through the kindness of God's dear people, both in Britain, and, in a small way, by the saints in Johannesburg, and by friends at the Cape. Money spent in this way, is surely not misspent. The children of Israel were exhorted by the Lord, in a certain connection, to remember that they were bondmen in the land of Egypt, and that the Lord God had redeemed them, therefore they should furnish their poor brethren liberally, with that wherewith He had blessed them in (Deut. xxvi. 12-13). It has been thought by some that a cure for leprosy can be reached by an entirely fruit diet. I believe from a scientific point of view, something might be said in favour of this theory. I knew a few on the Island who tried it for a while, and seemed to derive benefit therefrom, but the difficulty is to get a regular supply

ROBBEN ISLAND

of fruit through all the year. Personally, I am satisfied, that comparatively few people know the *real* value of lemons. However, I am afraid that something more than a mere fruit diet will be necessary, for the entire removal of leprosy from the system. As a matter of fact, doctors are well nigh at their wit's end regarding the Robben Island lepers. Every now and then, the Government has employed an expert for research work, and I have no doubt that these men have done their very utmost to find a cure for this malignant disease. But all to no purpose. As to the *causes* of leprosy, doctors know very little; that the disease is contagious, goes without saying. However, after twenty-four years experience, one is able to form an opinion, based upon much that I have seen and heard. Some little while back, an expert (Dr Sandes), on Robben Island, discovered that "a healthy person could be inoculated with this disease, through the *bite of a bed insect*, after sixteen days. In view of what this doctor says with reference to the leprous microbe, I am inclined to believe that the surest way of contracting the disease is, by inoculation. Still, how are we going to get rid of the fact that experiments have been so made on animals, birds, etc., without any evil results?

I noticed a printing frame lately hanging under a tree in the shade. On enquiring as to what this meant, I was told that " printing in the shade, marks or blemishes on the face, were to some extent removed." How many a poor sinner would like to have his inner man printed in the shade ! But God has portrayed him in the light (Rom. iii. 10-19). " He has been

TROPHIES OF GRACE AMONG THE LEPERS

weighed in the balances and found wanting " (Dan. v. 27).

June 1913.—I met on board an eminent doctor, whom I have known for some years past. On more than one occasion we have conversed on spiritual things, but to-day, I was able to come very near to him. I told him that I had long entertained the feeling that he was a true Christian. " Well, yes," he said, " I believe I am." I soon discovered that there were a few questions occupying his mind, such as Re-incarnation. " Had I heard of it ? " I replied that I had, but that I regarded such questions with great suspicion, and for years past had made a practice of testing everything I heard or read on religious matters, by the Word of God. Our conversation was renewed on the way back, and the doctor's interest was very manifest as I spoke to him of the coming of the Lord *for* the Church, and *with* the Church, remarking that these two comings must never be confused. Strange to say, when next I visited the Island, the doctor was again on board, and almost immediately referred to spiritual things, so that I have little question as to his being truly converted. What a cause it is for thankfulness in days of increasing darkness and scepticism, to meet with, and be able to help such men. " Not many mighty, not many noble." Some one once thanked God that it did not read, " Not ANY mighty, not ANY noble." Lady Huntingdon thanked God for the letter " M."

CHAPTER XIV.

"LONELY HEARTS TO CHERISH."

January 1914.—Around the old parish once more, and I trust, was able by God's grace, to cheer many a drooping spirit; such service among believers is alone more than enough to occupy one's time. "There are lonely hearts to cherish, as the days are going by." One dear fellow with tears in his eyes said, " I am so glad to see you, you have been such a help to me," He had just undergone an operation. He was born in Mexico, but lived in Port Elizabeth for some years, where he has a wife and family. He was formerly a Roman Catholic, but now assures me that he is resting on the finished work of Christ alone.

I was speaking to a native believer to-day, whose face shines like " a well-polished shaft." Yes, he can in measure say, " In the shadow of His hand hath He hid me, and made me a polished shaft " (Isa. xlviii. 2). He has been very ill since I last saw him, and has a silver tube now inserted in his windpipe, enabling him to breathe more freely, thus prolonging his life a little. He said with a face beaming with joy, and holding up a stumped finger, " I was as near to heaven as that, sir, but I was not afraid, for Jesus was quite near me."

February.—One day during this month, Dr M'Kay, from Durban, Natal, went over with me. I found him greatly interested in the patients, although he had never seen one before. I am sure he will put to good account, what he has seen to-day. He knew the specialist now engaged on the Island, so we called at his laboratory and saw him. It was extremely interesting to see his experiments on rats, mice, rabbits, etc., all with the hope of finding some remedy for this terrible disease.

9th March.—Mr Bull, who is here on a visit from Kimberley, joined me in a trip to the Island. This is his first acquaintance with the lepers, and as one might naturally expect, he was greatly impressed with the extent of the work. What struck him most was " not the loss of their hands and feet, which is the case with many, but their readiness to listen to the Word of God." Mr Bull was touched with some nice things a dear old Kaffir said, but it is necessary to be able to follow the native mind, to grasp the beauty of these. Mr D. Crawford shows this in his book *Thinking Black*. For instance Janjolo says, " My home is not here, but in heaven, and I am serving the Lord here, not in order to get to heaven, but because I shall not be able to do so in this manner, when I am there." What a beautiful thought from this dear leper. I am reminded of Eph. v. 16, " Redeeming the time, because the days are evil."

(I can " follow the native mind " sufficiently to " grasp the beauty " of the above quotation, which has proved an inspiration to me, many times.—W. H. Bull.)

Another dear fellow who is stone blind, asked me to repeat something I had said years ago, and which had been such a comfort to him. He said he had been thinking that if he had been given the choice to be either blind or deaf, he would have chosen the former, adding that faith cometh by hearing and not by seeing (Rom. x. 17).

June.—Work amongst the lepers is especially encouraging just now as there is a growing interest in the Gospel being manifested. This may to some extent be due to their having settled down to the inevitability of their unhappy lot. For years, they were kept in a state of suspense, apparently through lack of candidness on the part of the Goverment; not but what the patients have been treated with the greatest consideration by them. Hopes had, however, been held out to them that one day they would be removed to the mainland, but now they were told plainly, that no such hope can any longer be extended to them. So they know the worst now.

I met with an interesting case quite recently. " How could he be quite sure he was saved by just trusting the Lord Jesus ? " Adding that " people on the Island told him that sin was so very fine, that he might do something at the last moment and again be lost." " Oh, is that your difficulty ? " " Yes, sir." I then opened the Word and explained matters as best I could, leaving him, I believe, satisfied with what God's Word had to say on the question. Oh, what a commanding power and influence the Word of God has, over the human heart and mind. Thank God, we are not left to ourselves to settle these vital questions. I sent him the booklet, *Safety, Certainty and Enjoyment,* which I found had much helped him.

"LONELY HEARTS TO CHERISH"

Dear old Africander has gone to his eternal rest. He was an inmate in the Institute for twenty years. Blind, handless, and footless, for many years, his submissive will, his always peaceful, happy and contented life, spoke to the other patients. I often heard him say, " I have much to be thankful for." I wondered where he could find it ; certainly not on Robben Island, nor in himself, and he did not seek it there. Oh, what a blessed consolation to such, to know that ere long they shall awake in Christ's likeness, to see Him as He is, and to be for ever with Him. Yes, this corruptible must put on incorruption and this mortal immortality (1 Cor. xv. 53). Thank God, He is able to subdue all things unto Himself (Phil. iii. 21).

April 1915.—War between England and Germany has brought serious disturbances into Cape Colony, rebellion and strife being the most sad aspects. This, one regrets to find, has necessitated mobilization of the Defence forces, and the calling out of the loyal Burghers, so that my time has been fully taken up in visiting the various camps established along the Suburban Line. It has meant a very busy time for me, so that visits to the Island have been somewhat neglected. I am thankful, however, to say that my brother has gone on with the Robben Island work, visiting them every week, often twice, whilst I have gone over occasionally. I was surprised to find one day, when at the Docks, that twenty-five leper patients had come over, being sent back to their own homes on the mainland. One had been on the Island for forty-five years. Poor things, it must have been almost like

ROBBEN ISLAND

life from the dead to be released. They are returning on the ground that the disease is arrested.

May.—Mr W. Barton, who is here from Pondoland, went over with me to-day. It is not the first time that he has seen a leper, as there are a few in Pondoland. I was pleased to have him with me, because he was able to speak to the natives in their own language.

13th August 1915.—Joseph and I are kept very busy. Now and then, one goes on without stopping to eat. How can one do otherwise, when surrounded by hundreds who are ready to listen to the message, whose bodies are wasting away, and who may be in Eternity before long. How very great is our responsibility. I sometimes think of the words of the prophet when I look at those poor maimed bodies, " Son of man can these bones live ? " (Ezek. xxxvii. 3). All he could answer was, " Lord God, Thou knowest." But we have further light on the question when we turn to the New Testament. " He is able to subdue all things unto Himself " (Phil. iii. 21).

I met with a very sincere native believer to-day. He expressed to me his intense hatred of sin, of everything that is dishonouring to God. Really he made me feel very humble. I must admit that some of these native Christians are noble characters.

Several visits were made up to October, when we decided to erect a large tent at Salt River, where it was worked for two and half months, with Services every day. It was hard and trying work to keep it up at times, in the face of strong south-easterly gales.

22nd April 1916.—Mr W. Hoste, B.A., from England, went with me to-day, but, being Saturday, our time was very limited. Still, we were able to visit a few wards, and speak to individuals here and there. Mr Hoste was pleased with his visit, and much impressed as he watched some of the patients being treated, by the careful manner in which the attendants did it. To my mind, the risk these attendants run in handling the patients, even though strong disinfectants are used, is very great.

About the middle of May, Mr Anton, from Kalunda, Central Africa, went over with me. We had a very enjoyable day, and covered a lot of ground, giving a word here and there. We were told of a man in No. 10 Ward who was dying. We called and found him lying on his back with his mouth wide open, and both eyes closed. We were told that he was not conscious. I said to him in Dutch, " Mr Fish is standing by your bed." At once his eyes began to twitch, and in a few moments he was able to open them. I asked him if he knew me. " Yes." I quoted slowly and distinctly, several portions about the Blood. I questioned him if he was sure that he was under the shelter of the precious Blood. He assured me by clear signs that he was. This is one encouraging feature in the Dutch people. You are dealing with a people who from their childhood have been taught to believe in the Word of God. Mr Anton was very pleased to see the Lord's work amongst the lepers; there is nothing like a personal visit to beget real interest.

12*th May.*—Mr L. S. is slowly sinking, almost too weak to speak. I read a little from Peter's First Epistle, but did not remain long with him. Had a profitable time with a Kaffir in No. 4. Met a man in No. 10, who, with a number of other patients a year ago, was sent to B——; but he was so unhappy there that he wrote requesting the Government to allow him to return to the Island. I remember his conversion very well.

29th May.—On calling at Mr L's. room this morning, I learned that he had entered " The Banqueting Hall," and G. was occupying his room. I had a long talk with him about his stay in the B—— Institute. He told me that he had been very unhappy there, for there had been nothing but card-playing, dancing, and all kinds of worldliness from day to day, and he longed to be back on the Island again, where he could hear the Word of God. Just at that moment his food was brought in, and I suggested that he should take it whilst it was hot, but no, he preferred to have something for his soul. How very encouraging it is, to find such hungry souls over on Robben Island!

I called on Wiblin, a striking object of pity! He appeared glad to see me, but he soon began to lament his terrible affliction, showing me parts of his body. Oh, what an awful sight! I read the first two chapters of Job, and was wonderfully helped of God in applying much of it to him; but he is a hard case; still not too hard for God. I was kept busy answering questions until I had to leave for the steamboat, so ate my food on board, and enjoyed it all the more!

2nd June.—This is the second day that I have been over this week. One would need to go over every day to do anything like justice, to the work. A brother in the Lord, Mr Hansen, went with me. On our rounds we called on Wiblin, but he was in a bitter state of mind, so that we could do very little with him; he said that he had fully made up his mind to have nothing to do with God. I warned him solemnly as to the inevitable result of turning his back upon God, but finally we had to leave him.

Poor Greyling, he was suffering much, having undergone an operation for his eyes. One poor fellow wept bitterly, as we spoke to him of Christ.

2nd September.—Met with two very interesting cases to-day, but for want of more time had to leave them, partly helped; whereas if one were resident on the Island, they might have been brought to real decision of heart for Christ.

I saw a most touching sight when returning from the female location. A man was wheeling a poor leper woman in a little toy cart only about three feet long. She was doubled up like a bundle of filthy rags. She had no hands, no feet, and I think was blind! Oh, the ravages that are made, by this awful disease!

15th November.—I am surrounded by over six hundred poor lepers, suffering under various forms of the most terrible scourge, that the human body has ever been subject to. Something above the average nerve courage is required, to approach these poor souls. I have met with a few such to-day. There is, however, a peculiar joy and satisfaction in speaking to a poor leper of the love of God; one feels that one is following closely in the steps of the Master, Who, though so infinitely pure and holy, was humble enough

ROBBEN ISLAND

to approach, yea, even touch, a poor unclean leper (Luke v. 12). His, " be not weary," has sufficed in the past, and will do in the future. There is a strong gale blowing, so I expect it will be rough returning. But,

> " No wave ever beats on that beautiful shore,
> Where the tide of Eternity rolls."

Quite a number of patients are becoming blind; and this is having a depressing effect; they feel, as one told me to-day, that his last bit of comfort was going.

One very dear young believer, Lukas le Roux, told us that his eyesight was failing, and what he felt most was, that he would no longer be able to read the Word of God for himself, therefore he entreated us not to pass by his little room. We met an old blind man to-day, an intelligent believer. He has been on the Island many years. Poor old brother, he simply devours the Word! I intimated my intention of settling on the Island some day, if possible. The joy that filled his heart and found expression in his face, was most touching!

5th October 1917.—Have had the pleasure of seeing the dear lepers again. As a rule I am able to get over once a week, but it is about the last place in the world where the natural man would think of going. There is nothing on that Island to satisfy mere curiosity; everything from the leper standpoint is most repellent. Just now there are some very sad cases; one staggers at the awful condition of some of them. A perfect description of them is found in Isa. i. 6.

I have been dealing with a man lately, who has

"LONELY HEARTS TO CHERISH"

lived a rough life; there is not a sound spot in the whole of his body. He is humbled and broken before God; he owns himself a vile sinner, but cannot rise and trust in the Lord. He feels like Cain of old, that " his iniquity is greater than can be taken away " (mar.) (Gen, iv. 13).

3rd December.—I met with a few very nice cases to-day, who were, I believe, helped to a clearer understanding of God's simple plan of salvation. Oh, what patience one needs in dealing with minds so utterly void of a true knowledge of God!

J. B. told me again of his conversion. How that he was more or less under conviction when brought to Robben Island. That I had given him a copy of *God's way of Salvation,* in Dutch, which he read with much interest, and was soon fully convinced of his need of salvation, but not only so, he saw also from that little book, that it was possible to possess it now. So there and then, he decided for Christ.

I had a very earnest word with G. B., and I have reason to believe that God has at last delivered that precious soul from the very jaws of death. Before leaving, and after a long talk with him about his soul, I put the question solemnly to him, " May I now thank God that you have at last accepted Christ as your Saviour ? " Without the slightest hesitation he replied, " Yes, Mr Fish, you can." He is truly a brand plucked out of the fire (Zec. iii. 2). For months past I have sought the Lord earnestly for this dear man, and I am sure that my brother has also. But we are so rarely together on the Island, that I have no idea what his impression of him is. He has a sister

ROBBEN ISLAND

there, whom Joseph often deals with ; a most pitiable object for human eyes. To-day, just before entering the ward, I got aside in a quiet spot and asked the Lord to give me the right word for that young fellow. And it is really wonderful how God wrought. I met a sad case in No. 1, a man of the name of Johnson. Poor fellow, he is in a wretched condition, and can only last a few days. I am ashamed to say, that I sometimes feel like the Priest and the Levite, I have to " pass by on the other side." Thank God, not for want of love and compassion, but for lack of physical nerve !

10th December.—A profitable time with the patients. I met a young man in No. 1, who is evidently nearing his end. His poor broken-hearted mother, who had been allowed to visit him, was standing by his bed seeking to soothe her boy. I felt I could do little, beyond quoting a few well-known verses of Scripture. Near his bed was a young native, whom I found quite ready to listen to the message, and I have reason to believe that he was definitely helped.

I am convinced that personal dealing with souls is the more excellent way of reaching these poor lepers. It is most interesting to watch the effect of God's Word upon a soul ; light enters into the mind and heart, revealing and dispelling the darkness, and then implanting therein the true Life and Light, bringing joy and gladness.

I met an old blind man, and said to him : " I see you have lost your natural sight; what about the eyes of your heart, are they blind also ? " He replied, " No." " What then is the most important thing

These are little huts the Government allows them to make, and live in during the day. Myself standing partly inside speaking to four native women, Xosas, nearly all are without hands and feet.

(1) About to extract a tooth. (2) Leaving for Lusikisiki, my native boy standing by.

"LONELY HEARTS TO CHERISH"

you have ever seen with these eyes?" His lovely answer was "Jesus on the Cross for me." After a further conversation with him, I found he was a true believer in Christ. The last one I saw to-day was G. B., who accepted Christ as his Saviour last Monday. I found him still trusting, calm, and happy, reminding me of Mark v. 15. "Sitting and clothed, and in his right mind." After reading 1 Peter i. 3 to 7, and exhorting him to keep his eyes upon the Lord, not upon himself, I quoted a few verses from a well-known Dutch hymn, and left him. Poor fellow! as to his body, he is one open ulcer from head to foot.

5th January 1918.—It was rather foggy going over this morning, but the sea was calm. Saw Lucas; had a nice talk with him over the Word. It is most encouraging to see the intelligence of this young man, and he is not able to read a single word, being stone blind. He is always very grateful for our visits to him. Poor B.! He is indeed a pitiable object to behold! One needs a strong nerve to look on such cases. I am glad, however, that he knows Christ as his Saviour now. Oh, how changed the expression on that poor disfigured face! He says, " It is all too wonderful." I told of the grand change which would be ours, should the Lord come, while I was still in his room. Spoke to many others before leaving. Oh, for the grace to value more highly these golden opportunities!

25th January.—My brother and I had a very good time as usual, with the patients. Whilst speaking to a few men in front of one of the wards, another came along and, after listening for a time, he boldly con-

ROBBEN ISLAND

fessed Christ as his Saviour, and also appealed to the others as to how far they could testify to such a blessed hope. We found B. still calmly resting on Christ. Like the words of the hymn:

> " Jesus I am resting, resting, in the joy of what Thou art;
> I am finding out the greatness of Thy loving heart.
> Thou hast bid me gaze upon Thee, and Thy beauty fills my soul.
> For by Thy transforming power, Thou hast made me whole."

Poor little boy Heins in the next cubicle! The condition of his body can scarcely be described. He is only twelve years old, but he is a happy little child of God, enduring his trial bravely.

I never knew the work on Robben Island more encouraging than it is at the present time. There is a real spirit of enquiry all round, and some who have recently been brought to the Lord are confessing Him, before others.

28th.—Was at Stickland for a week-end Service. Went straight from my brother's house to the Island. Mr Hill of Wellington was to have gone with me, but he did not turn up. Perhaps it was as well he did not, as it has been very rough. Met with a poor fellow in No. 1, evidently near his end. So far as I could judge from a few questions put to him, he was prepared to go. It is most touching to witness a poor leper dying. Few indeed are his comforts in this world, fewer still his sympathisers. The only one near his bed to render him any assistance was a poor fellow, with both hands and feet rotting off. True there is a staff of warders provided by Government, but they are very limited, so that it is impossible

"LONELY HEARTS TO CHERISH"

to give patients all the attention they require. I met with a sad case in No. 2. Oh, the awful ignorance regarding the most simple truths of the Bible ! It makes one feel sad. Had a peep at B. before I left; he is a little better in some respects. Poor little Pete, as we call him ! I said to him to-day, " Well, Pete, how did you enjoy the peaches I sent you ? " His poor little disfigured face began to beam with joy. I have never yet beheld sadness on that little fellow's face. I am afraid that could not be said of many of us, notwithstanding our many blessings.

6th February.—We have had another day of happy service on the island. Mr Eachus went with me. He was deeply interested ; and I am inclined to think that God blessed a conversation he had with one man. We called and saw Mr T. ; there we met another man who had just been brought to the Island. He told us that he had developed leprosy in German South-West Africa, during the war campaign. In course of conversation, Mr T. told us of a very valuable discovery made for leprosy, by a certain doctor, now on the Island, which was likely to prove a real cure. This opened up an opportunity to speak to them of God's perfect remedy for sin. We touched at No. 10. Saw little Pete for a moment; poor little fellow, his condition is enough to soften a heart of stone. Saw B. in the next cubicle for a few moments ; what a picture to behold ; bandaged from head to foot, it takes an attendant about two hours to renew his bandages. And yet there he is, after a long struggle with the devil, a wondrous trophy of grace, " Waiting for the adoption, to wit, the redemption of his body "

ROBBEN ISLAND

(Rom. viii. 23). After taking a little refreshment, we proceeded to Murray's Bay, where the females are housed. We found Miss S. very happy in the knowledge of her sins forgiven; the poor girl is quite blind. We met with a few Kaffir men and women sitting under some trees, to whom we spoke of God's love, and at the close sang one or two hymns in Kaffir. We then visited the huts at the top of the Island, where we could have easily spent the whole of our time, without touching the wards at all. Dear Susie Abbot, the released slave from the Zambesi, is fully confident that she will one day be in the glory.

13th February.—I have experienced one of the hottest days on the Island to-day, that I have known for many years. It was really painful to watch some of the dear patients gasping for breath, especially those who have the silver tube in the windpipe. Young Mr John Hynd went with me to-day, and was deeply touched by the sights. On leaving, he said, " That he would never to the end of his days, forget his visit to that Island; " and yet it was very little I could show him in the few hours we had there. As we behold some of God's dear children so sorely afflicted, we can only exhort them to look up, " For the coming of the Lord draweth nigh."

3rd April.—Have been prevented more or less from going to the Island of late, but I am glad to be able to visit the patients once more. The boat that runs regularly is laid up, so we were obliged to go over in a small motor launch; fortunately it was fine weather, otherwise I should not have ventured. It has been very warm to-day, which made it hard work to go round. Poor B. still lingers, and also little Pete. Poor boy! it made me feel sick looking at what one time might have been called hands : but words of mine fail to describe what they are like to-day, yet these two are both happy in knowing Jesus as their Saviour. I heard to-day that the Dutch Reformed minister would be leaving on Friday, and I hope a good man will be appointed in his place, as I sincerely believe that there are souls yet to be saved, on the Island.

3rd August 1918.—I was cheered in one respect, to find poor B. and little Klaas Heins still in the body. Oh, what objects of pity ! and yet still happy in the Lord ! I apologised to Klaas for intruding upon him whilst he was taking his food, but he would not listen to that, and at once put aside his plate, and in effect said, " A visit from you is more to me than my food." I at once settled down and read to him from the Word of God. I told him that his position reminded me of Noah, when he was shut up in the Ark with his family: all around was darkness and death, no bright spot to be seen anywhere, except in one direction, and that was heavenward; he, too, could see nothing on Robben Island but gloom and death (a living death), but he could always look above and by faith see the One who came down to earth, and died to bring him to God. Poor B. in the next cubicle was calm and confident. Had a nice time speaking to him, and closed with a word of prayer. I spoke to several others ; one young man who joined up and had been to France had now returned a leper, having developed the disease during his absence there. I believe one young lad was decidedly helped to-day ;

ROBBEN ISLAND

to God be the glory! I felt quite upset in watching an attendant dress the foot of a patient.

9th August.—I shall bless God for all Eternity for being allowed to bring His Glad Tidings to these poor lepers on Robben Island. It is just in such sad surroundings that one sees the triumphs of that blessed Gospel, not only in saving souls, but enabling them also to rejoice in the midst of such depressing circumstances. One sees on that Island to-day, those who once lived most ungodly lives, now calmly sitting at the feet of the Saviour. I have been speaking to one such to-day. Poor Gert B., the man who only a little while ago was as dark as midnight, and despaired of ever being saved, is now a marvellous trophy of grace. His poor sister is even worse than himself; as a matter of fact she is almost unapproachable. I have often remarked that a personal visit to the Island alone will help visitors to a clear understanding of their condition. There you can see the disease in all stages of its development.

19th August.—I have had the pleasure of Lieut. Arnold's company to-day, and I believe God has been pleased to make him a blessing to more than one of the poor lepers. He has an excellent way in my opinion of dealing with individuals; he uses wonderful tact. I was glad to hear Lucas say, with reference to what Mr Arnold had brought before him, touching the *power* of the *Gospel* in the past, " Yes, and the Lord is the same to-day." When about to leave him, he said to Mr Arnold, " I want to ask you one thing, Sir; will you pray for this Island ? " One felt assured of the sincerity of his request, as

"LONELY HEARTS TO CHERISH"

he heaved a sigh and shook his head, saying : " There are many on the Island not yet saved. I have been blind for two years, but, Oh, God has taught me more in these two years, than I ever learned in all my life before."

It was interesting to hear Mr Arnold explain to poor little Pete, the wonderful change from the chrysalis to the beautiful butterfly, and apply it to the boy ; showing the change that his body would undergo, at the Lord's coming. He spoke of his spirit being imprisoned in that awful, corrupting body, just waiting to come out ! We saw poor B. for a few minutes, then went to No. 1, passed quickly through, took a little refreshment, and hurried down to the females, spoke to one here and there, but subsequently settled down in No. 8, where we met with a nice young European woman, May de Ruck, who had only been five months on the Island. After finding that she was able to understand English, I got Mr Arnold to speak to her, and I must say we had a most interesting time, leaving her, I believe, fully trusting in the Lord. Mr Arnold had an interesting time too, with Major W., who also came from London ; so that they were able to talk freely of places they knew. He has been ten years on the Island a leper, and is now blind. I am not sure if he is on the Rock of Ages ; however, I believe Mr Arnold was a help to him.

2nd September.—It is a beautiful morning ; " a morning without clouds." The sun shines brightly, though the past month (which is usually stormy) was conspicuous by the absence of rain and strong winds ; indeed, I never remember such a dry, calm, and warm August. We are now on our way back from the Island. (I often make notes on the boat.) I have not been able to deal with many to-day, nevertheless I have had a good time with a few. After all it is the *quality* of work we want, and not the quantity we aim at. B. was very low, nearly gone, but the Lord has had mercy on him, and restored him again. I had a nice talk with Mr T., and he pressed me to call and see him again when I come over, adding, " you are welcome to come at any time." This is encouraging, when we remember who he is. Leaving him I called on May de Ruck. I said to her: " Well, May, are you happy ? " " Yes," was her reply. " What makes you happy, May ? " " Because I am saved." I thought this was a very simple answer, and very clear. I then tried, from the Word, to help her a little further, and I believe she was encouraged to confess Christ as her Saviour before the others. This is the young girl who professed to be saved when Mr Arnold was with me. I met a very nice Kaffir to-day who assures me, that he is trusting in Jesus. I feel specially drawn to the dear natives ; as a rule they are most sincere, when once they are saved.

14th September.—There was a light breeze, but a heavy swell. My brother and I found that four fresh cases had been taken over. Alas ! that there are those still found in the Colony to take the places of the many who die ; and so the old standard number of over six hundred is kept up. Dear Nellie B. was buried to-day. I was present at the Burial Service, which was conducted in Dutch, by the Dutch Reformed minister. Deut. xxx. 9 to end was read, and parts of

"LONELY HEARTS TO CHERISH"

two Dutch hymns sung. The most one can say is, that the address was suited to a believer. A few helpful remarks were made for Christians, but nothing for the unsaved who stood round. Moses had an object in life, and he reached out after that, calmly meeting all the opposing influences of darkness. He was alone at the end, yet not alone, for God was with him. The minister, at the close of his address, asked me if I had been able to follow him. I told him that I had clearly followed him, but what one felt as of primary importance is, to make the way to life plain *first*, quoting Rom. vi. last verse. He said in his address, that " Nellie had reached her goal." Thank God, she had, but never reached it by any efforts of her own. What a happy release! As to her body, she was one of the most pitiable cases Robben Island has ever seen, and yet she possessed that calm confidence in God's Word, coupled with amazing patience. The disease, during the last two weeks that she lingered, developed to such an extent, that it was almost impossible to approach her at all, and yet she found some consolation in thinking of others worse than herself. She has a brother in a similar condition; and he also is trusting in the Lord.

It is sad to witness any funeral service, but I always feel that it is doubly sad to see a poor leper buried, when the only sympathizers they have are just like themselves. " Lord, how long shall the wicked, how long shall the wicked triumph?" (Psa. lxciv. 3).

CHAPTER XV.

A TERRIBLE SCOURGE.

October 1918.—We have just been visited by a terrible epidemic, known as the " Spanish Flu," which at the present moment is raging throughout the Colony like wild-fire, carrying off thousands, both rich and poor. Some of the principal business places have had to close down, for want of a sufficient staff to carry on. During the height of this fearful scourge, not less than two hundred and fifty corpses were conveyed by train daily, to a local cemetery just outside Cape Town, to say nothing of those taken to the suburban cemeteries, including Wynberg, where not less than a hundred and fifty new graves were made daily, and where on several occasions I was engaged in holding Funeral Services. A brother in the Lord told me, that when leaving his house one morning, he saw men bring out of one house, and lay upon a waggon, not less than twelve dead bodies !

I was deeply impressed one day, whilst waiting at the entrance to the Wynberg Cemetery for a funeral party. A large military procession with band, officers, and guns, came along conveying the body of the one who had been the chief nurse at the Military Camp, and for this everything else had to stand aside. There was also an ordinary brick cart with two bodies thereon rolled up in blankets, coffins being out of the

A TERRIBLE SCOURGE

question, unless the relatives could make them out of paraffin boxes. Standing on one side of the gate was what made a touching picture ; an ass with its little burden : some loved one being borne to his or her last resting place. Oh, how vividly the scene passed before my mind, when on that most memorable occasion our Lord rode into Jerusalem on the colt of an ass. Glorious burden ! He who had come, and now " hath abolished death, and hath brought life and immortality to light through the Gospel." But the most pathetic sight of all, and the one which touched me to the heart, was a poor man, looking as pale as death, bearing on his shoulder a little roughly made coffin, containing, no doubt, his own darling child ! And to crown the picture, walking behind were two little barefooted children, a boy and a girl, with tiny bunches of daisies in their hands. What a contrast to the great military procession ! Then came the cortege for which I waited. The body was to be buried in what is commonly known as " consecrated ground," but the minister, having far more than he could well attend to, permitted me to go on with the Burial Service.

On another occasion, in a different cemetery, having to conduct a Service, as I stood at the end of the grave, I found myself at the back of a Church of England minister, who was also conducting a Service. We waited until he had finished ; and as I was about to read a passage of Scripture, the friends next to us commenced to sing the well-known hymn, " Abide with me." I suggested to our brethren not to stand on ceremony, so we all joined in and sang it through.

ROBBEN ISLAND

The whole thing was a perfect Babel! A large piece of ground at the end of the Cemetery had been cleared for the purpose, and it seemed to me like, " first come, first served," drop your corpse down into the first hole you come to. What with the singing, weeping, and howling, it made one's brain whirl. And so I might go on, telling of those awful days. Thank God! although in the very thick of it, we have been marvellously preserved; neither my dear wife nor I have had a single attack. I might add, that notwithstanding the fact that all the patients on Robben Island, some hundreds, were laid low by this terrible scourge, only eleven died during this time.

13th December 1918.—My brother and I were over to-day, and, as usual, had a good time with the lepers. It certainly is very encouraging just now, for there is a marked interest in the Gospel, on all sides. I believe that many are beginning to find out that mere formal religion can never save their souls. They see now that " None but Christ can satisfy," so those who have been led to trust in the Lord, are, as a rule, especially bright.

It is sad to find such a number of them becoming blind. This makes it more incumbent on us to visit them as often as possible, but we are amply rewarded for any self-sacrifice made by their deep appreciation of our visits. One might say of a few : " To them every bitter thing is sweet." There is a real hungering and thirsting for the Word of God. Poor things, what else have they on that dismal Island to cheer them ?

20th January 1919.—I expected Mr A. to go with

A TERRIBLE SCOURGE

me this morning, but he did not put in an appearance, so I had to go alone. There was a strong wind blowing, and we had a good drenching going off in the motor launch, but when compared with the great privilege and joy which is ours in bringing the glad tidings to such a sorrow-stricken people, it is as nothing, and soon forgotten. Oh, to be found worthy of God, and in such a condition that He can use me! "A vessel sanctified and meet for the Master's use." The Apostle in writing to the Thessalonian saints, not only called them to witness to the power of the Gospel that he had preached amongst them, but also to his manner of life, which they very well knew. Surely this is of much in importance in the Christian life, and I feel the need of its being pressed home upon my own heart, as well as upon others. I am afraid that many of us are not too much concerned regarding the testimony of the outside world. "They themselves show," said the Apostle, "concerning us, what manner of entering in we had among you." Here we have the testimony of those without, who saw the work of grace in the Thessalonian Saints.

29*th January*.—Moved around amongst the male patients in the morning, and went to Murray's Bay in the afternoon. Among others I saw Miss de Ruck, and urged upon her the necessity of a careful consistent walk before her fellow-patients, pointing out to her that the world pays more attention to the life of a Christian, than to his preaching. The former apart from the latter will have little influence.

10*th February*.—I was glad of Mr Arnold's company. We called on Dr Moon, who kindly allowed us to visit the Mental Asylum. It made me sad as I saw poor Frank sitting on the side of his bed, tearing his shirt to pieces. This young man was brought to the Lord during the Spanish Flu. One is at a loss, sometimes, to understand some of God's dealings with us, but faith bows before such an all-wise and loving God, and awaits the issues of His will.

We then called on Major W., and had a very profitable conversation about the Lord. I am inclined, after all, to believe that the Major is trusting in the finished work of Christ. My brother has laboured hard for this dear soul, and I do trust that it will be found in *that day*, that he has not laboured in vain.

We spoke to many others during the day, finishing up with a word with poor Susie Abbot. Mr Arnold had committed to memory a short sentence in Dutch and he made good use of it—one of the " fitalls," it came in anywhere, so when we were leaving Susie " Tot wederziens " (good-bye till I see you again), came in as a last good-bye as far as this life is concerned. He is about to return to England, so that the next meeting may be in the clouds!

7th April 1919.—I had a most enjoyable time, and felt like going on without any refreshment. Oh, how easy it is to speak even in a strange tongue when the joy of the Lord fills one's heart. The truth of the Lord's return was very much before me to-day, arising chiefly from two questions in 1 Cor. xv. verse 35. These two questions are answered in the same chapter; verses 51 to 54 provide the answer to the first, and verses 42 to 44 to the second. I gave most of my time to believers in visiting to-day.

A TERRIBLE SCOURGE

After visiting several of the wards, I called and saw Mr G. W. in his private room. He was looking remarkably well, and told me that he was expecting to leave the Island soon for a place named St Raphael's Home, Faure. This farm has been purchased, I believe, by the Church of England, who provide a home for any in whom the disease has been arrested. He said he could have left the Island five years ago but refused. He has been twenty-four years here. I asked him to what he attributed the improvement in his body. He said " Well, Mr Fish, if I may give you an answer from Scripture, then I must say, This is the Lord's doing, it is marvellous in our eyes." This was surely a nice answer. He reminded me of the condition of his body many years ago, " Wounds, bruises, and putrefying sores." He said that Robben Island had been to him something like the Isle of Patmos was to John. I told him if he had learned ever so little of what was revealed to John on that Island, he had learned much. He replied, " that it had been his earnest prayer to God all along that He would cure him if it might be for His glory, otherwise he was quite contented to remain on the Island for the rest of his days." He is quite blind.

14th *April.*—The joy of seeing the patients again was mine to-day. Poor Rechter is gone. I say " poor "—he is rich indeed. Two years before he died, he was " poor and needy," but since then he has shown a true work of grace in his heart. Lucas will miss him very much, as they were often together and enjoyed sweet fellowship in the things of God. It was a real inspiration to one's soul as we neared their room, to see their poor disfigured faces shine, at the very sound of our voices. Oh, may we never lose sense of the great privilege which is ours, in being allowed to visit these poor lepers with God's blessed Gospel!

30th April.—Had a happy and busy time, so that I took nothing to eat before I came back to the boat. Enjoyed a conversation with B. and Small, also with G. W. Spent the rest of my time in No. 1 Ward, and met with an interesting case there, a European confined to bed. After speaking to him for some time, he asked if I would explain what the new birth meant. I then went into a lengthy explanation of the subject, the result being that he was very much helped. He is above the average white Africander for intelligence, and I hope to find him happy in the Lord when I see him again. We have noticed a growing desire on the part of many of the patients, to listen to the Gospel. This is encouraging to us; formerly it was by no means easy work. Once we are satisfied that they are truly saved, we then bring before them the blessed truth of the Lord's coming to the air for the saints, as there is no other hope for them in this life. A cure for their malignant disease is altogether out of the question. (It is the one outstanding disease beyond all others for which no cure has ever yet been found, nor do I think ever will be, as for some purpose, it is not permitted by God.)

7th May.—Called on Mr Malan and Lucas this morning, enjoyed a talk with them, then passed through No. 1. This is the Hospital Ward, where so many are confined to their beds. Later, went to Murray's Bay. Met with two women, in a little hut.

Three lepers, with my sister-in-law, Mrs Joseph Fish. The patient standing is an exceedingly bright Christian.

A group of lepers, several believers among them. Little Dorothy du Wal next to the man on left; I am at the back on right.

Two native women sitting at the entrance of their little hut, with fingers gone, eating bread.

A TERRIBLE SCOURGE

Had a good time with them, and I have reason to think one was definitely helped. I then went to Susie's hut, and found her squatting on the ground outside, with a lot of ducks around her. "Well, Susie, how are you?" "Very well, sir." Can you conceive such a reply, when you remember that she has neither hands nor feet. I said to her, "Some day you will have a better body than that, Susie." I told her what the Bible says about an "incorruptible body," a "glorified body," a "powerful body," and a spiritual body. Her face literally shone with joy!

12th May.—Had a nice conversation with J. B. He told me that he deeply appreciated my visits to him, and always felt helped in his spiritual life as a result. Saw Mr Y. for a little while; I do not think he knows the Lord. He has a wife and two children living in W.; it is this separation from their loved ones that makes it so hard for these lepers.

One believer was very anxious to have some things explained to him with reference to the coming of the Lord. It is very noticeable in these days, how many Christians are being awakened to the "Blessed Hope." I met a fine, healthy-looking man to-day; he has been on the Island only three months. His name is Goes. He came from the leper location outside Pretoria, where he was an inmate for three years. He and another patient escaped from the asylum, but returned again the same day. However, they have both been sent to Robben Island as a sort of punishment, and their wives will not be allowed to see them for at least a year. There are over a hundred Europeans in the Pretoria Asylum, and nearly six

ROBBEN ISLAND

hundred coloured. I had an earnest word with Goes about his soul, but I found him like many more; quite ready to speak of God as his Father. It is really astonishing how many there are who know little or nothing of the A.B.C. of the Gospel.

20th May.—On the second and third Tuesday in the month the boat makes a special trip, for the benefit of any resident on the Island who wishes to come to Cape Town on business. The boat leaves the Docks at 8 a.m., and leaves the Island at 5 p.m. So for the first time I have taken advantage of this special boat, in order to have a long day amongst the patients. Of course it meant starting from Wynberg rather early. I have thoroughly enjoyed the day, and have been able to deal with a fair number. I was just twelve hours away from home. Met dear old Susie, again sitting outside her hut. I said to her, " Susie, if I were able, I would at once give you new hands and feet." " Well, sir," she replied, " perhaps if I had my hands and my feet, I might forget God, like so many I see on the Island, who have hands and feet, but seldom think of God." I was much touched by her humble reply. I exhorted her to be patient a little longer, when she would receive her glorified body. One patient carried me back in thought twenty-four years ago, " when," said he, " we looked eagerly forward to your weekly visits. I fancy I can see you now coming along from the boat." (He has been blind for many years.) We spoke of the conversion of some in those days. I enquired about Schalkwyk (this was the man who said that God had saved him with both hands).

A TERRIBLE SCOURGE

He told me that he had been sent from the Island three months ago, and had died in the Old Somerset Hospital, quite recently. I felt sorry that I did not know he was there, otherwise I would have visited him. He is without a doubt at home with the Lord, freed for ever from his misery. This dear old man went regularly every morning to the top of the Island, and there behind a bush communed with his God.

28th May.—I have to-day dealt mostly with unsaved persons ; one case which interested me much being that of a Roman Catholic. After asking and being told where he came from, I said to him : " In all probability you will never leave this Island again, until you are called from time into eternity, and there are two conditions, eternal happiness, or eternal misery. You and I are bound for one or the other of these two places. If you are a Christian, you are on your way to the first ; if not, you are going to the second. Now ! are you a Christian ? " He promptly replied, " Yes." " How long have you been a Christian ? " " Thirty-three years." " Thirty-three years ? " " Yes." " You must have been saved when you were very young. How old are you now ? " " Thirty-three years." " Oh ! " I said, " my friend you are making a great mistake. May I ask you how you became a Christian ? " " Some water was sprinkled on my head, and a cross made on my forehead." " Is that how you became a Christian ? " I asked. " Yes." " Then there was no need of the death of Christ in your case." Poor man ! he seemed to be in a sort of quagmire ; he had no solid foundation to stand upon. I spoke to him for nearly an hour, opening up the truth of the Cross. I was glad to find afterwards that he had a New Testament with him, and that he was reading it.

2nd June.—Had a talk with J. B. to-day, from Gen. xiii., setting forth the pursuits of life. It is important to observe where we pitch our tent. Lot pitched his tent toward *Sodom,* hence a wasted and sorrowful life. Not so with Abraham, who left the planning of his life to God. It reminds one of the man of Jer. xvii. 7. " His trust was in the Lord, he was as a tree planted by the waters, spreading out his roots by the river, his leaves ever green, neither did cease from yielding fruit." But Lot was the man of verses 5 and 6. He trusted in man, made flesh his arm, and his heart departed from the Lord. B. told me that he felt the need of more pureness of life, as he did not want any one to say to him, after he had spoken to them about the Lord, " What about your own life ? " He said if I saw anything wrong in his life, I was to tell him, and not to be afraid that he might get angry, as some people do. At the close of a little conversation with poor blind Georgie W., he told me that he had now received a spiritual feast. He regretted that he had not read the Bible more, when he had his eyesight. I had a profitable time with several others, especially with two Kaffirs, one practically without hands and feet. It was very touching to witness one of them struggling to eat his food. Oh, for a grateful heart to praise God for health !

30th July.—What with a sharp attack of rheumatism in my left foot, and stormy weather, my dear wife did not think it wise for me to go to the

A TERRIBLE SCOURGE

Island to-day, yet somehow I felt constrained to go, so I went. My foot certainly was very sore, and prevented me walking far on the Island. However, after calling on a few private patients, I proceeded towards the top of the Island, where I sat behind a bush to eat my bit of food. I had scarcely finished eating, when a patient came to me, and after asking one or two questions, he sat down on the ground. He then told me that he was in trouble regarding his soul; which I soon discovered was true. He had asked the Lord to pardon him, and hoped that He would do so some day. I said, " My friend, if you were a father, and your child asked you for something he badly needed, and which you were able and willing to give, how long would you keep him waiting ? " " Oh, I would give it at once," was his reply. " Just so. Then does not God give life eternal to those who believe on His Son ? You say you have cried to God, and He has heard, but you have been looking in the wrong direction for His answer. You have been looking into your own heart, instead of listening to what God's Word says." I then turned to several plain passages of Scripture, which were a help to him. After all, there is nothing that can help us in our troubles like the Word of God. It has a supreme command over the human heart and mind, as nothing else can have. He said, " I will hold fast to those Scriptures." " Yes, hold fast to the Word of God: that never changes, and don't mind your feelings." He asked very sincerely if it was possible to know that he possessed eternal life, before he died. I said, " Yes, most emphatically you can know." This

ROBBEN ISLAND

seemed to comfort him very much, and I believe he went away trusting in Christ as his personal Saviour.

11th August.—I half expected to find the self-propelling bath-chair on the Island to-day, but it had not turned up. Had a good time with the patients.

18th August.—Was glad to meet my brother at the Docks, and to find that he was also going over, as I had learned that the chair would be sent to-day. I had already arranged to have a photo. of the chair taken with a patient sitting in it, my brother and I standing by the side. The chair was sent to No. 10 Ward, where I had the first trial trip, and as you may suppose I soon found myself in a sort of quandary, but after a little floundering about, I saw that the entire machine was controlled by the one lever; it did remind me, nevertheless, of my first attempt to ride a bicycle. A few of the patients tried it afterwards, and succeeded very well, considering that some of them have very little hand left to grasp the handle; many of them no hands at all. I am trying to contrive some means whereby they can have their wrists fastened to the handles. How sad all this is! One may well ask, " What has the fall of man not brought upon this poor world ? " Thank God, it will not always be so. In the meantime, one has the privilege of proclaiming God's perfect remedy for sin *now*, and the promise of a glorified body, bye and bye. This self-propelling bath-chair has been graciously provided by dear Miss Alexander and her friends of Belfast, Ireland.

17th August.—Mr James MacPhie from Kazombo, Central Africa, went over with me and was much

A TERRIBLE SCOURGE

interested in what he saw of the work, though one gets only a faint idea in one short visit. We could only hurry through a few of the wards. I found to-day that there had been a little friction between the white and coloured patients; the latter thinking that they would not have free access to the bath-chair. I rather anticipated this, and saw the advisability of getting another for them. I believe in due time it will be forthcoming. I think the chair will be a help, enabling many who cannot walk, to get out into the open air.

24th August.—Joseph went down to the females; I remained among the men, and we both had a profitable time. The two brothers, Small, were in bed, badly afflicted. Oh, this terrible scourge, what ravages it has caused! And yet the work of grace in some dear souls, shines out brightly through it all. I enjoyed a conversation with Mr W., on the change of the believer's body at the coming of the Lord. The passage I read was 2 Cor. v. He said that he had never understood it so clearly before, and that I had given him food for thought.

3rd October.—There was a heavy swell on, and as usual several were unwell. On such days, much care must be exercised in landing the passengers at the jetty. Through the goodness of God, we have been wonderfully preserved through all these years, never having met with an accident, though knocked about sometimes by the sea, especially in the early days when we were landed on the beach and carried through the surf on the natives' shoulders. But when we remember the purpose of our visits, then winds and waves have little thought with us.

ROBBEN ISLAND

Among others spoken to to-day, were two patients in No. 2 Ward. One a Kaffir, the other an Africander. Both were fairly intelligent, but for want of more time I had to leave them. Hope (D.V.) to renew the conversation with them next week. There is one thing about the pure native, that is most encouraging, *i.e.* his sincerity.

10th October.—Was on the Island again, this week, but did not come in touch with the Kaffir boy, as he was away on another part of the Institute.

8th March 1920—I was favoured with the company of Mr Pugh from Mansfield, Natal, to-day. I was very pleased to have him with me, especially because he is acquainted with the native language, and was therefore a real help to the Kaffirs. A nice number came together in No. 2 Ward, and Mr Pugh spoke to them for about an hour. They were highly pleased to have some one to address them in their own tongue. Mr Pugh was satisfied with the answers some of the women gave to his questions. One question was, " What is the Lord doing now ? " the answer was, " He is perfecting our holiness."

Mr Pugh had an interesting talk with Mr T., and before he had finished, Mr T. found himself in rather a tight corner ; however, the result was, that he promised to read the new Testament. Altogether we had a very profitable day.

14th April.—Yesterday Mr George Lammond from Kaleba, and Mr Judson from Kaponga went with me. This was their first visit, so they were naturally impressed by the misery and suffering they saw there. It is a terrible sight for one who has never seen a

A TERRIBLE SCOURGE

leper, to gaze upon over six hundred poor creatures, with bodies decaying away. It requires a little more than ordinary nerve to deal with some of them. For instance, a man I saw yesterday confined to bed, his poor body in an advanced stage of decay, was so covered with flies that after speaking with him for a few moments I had to leave. Oh, for a deepening sense of gratitude in our hearts toward God, for preservation from such a terrible disease! When one considers for a moment the many years we have been allowed to visit these poor lepers, and not to have contracted the disease, I feel profoundly grateful. I was struck with the remark of one man yesterday. After speaking very plainly to him about his need of a Saviour, he said something to this effect, " If there were a few more like yourself stationed on the Island, the atmosphere would soon be changed."

30*th April*.—It is now over thirty years since we made our first trip to the Island, and we are glad to think, as a result of all those years of happy service among the poor lepers, that many will one day be in the glory, and shine out in the beauty of the Lord (2 Thess. i. 10). We passed a large shark on our way this morning. We were told that it is about eighteen feet long—a real man-eater. The fishermen have been trying to catch it for days past. Poor Botha! It was difficult to come near him this morning on account of the flies feasting on his open ulcers; and yet he is ever ready to " count his blessings "; which is really an inspiration. Next to his room lives Mr C., an Englishman; he has *written on his door*, outside, " Cosy Corner." I told him I did not know that it

ROBBEN ISLAND

was possible to find such a place on Robben Island! He said, " I have spent some of the happiest moments of my life in this room." He asked if I knew where the large water tanks are at the top of the Island. I said, " Yes." " Well," he replied, " that spot is like the Holy of Holies to me." What he really meant I can scarcely grasp; at any rate he seems to be able to turn the " Valley of Baca (weeping) into a well!" (Psa. lxxxiv. 6).

10th May.—I had the pleasure of taking Mr Colin Campbell of Edinburgh, to the Island to-day. The weather was fine, but there was a swell on. We spoke to a number of both saved and unsaved. We were, however, unable to make much headway with one man. He was so convinced that 1. Peter iii. 18, 19, offered a second hope, or another chance for man after this life. Of course we pointed out to him that that passage did not apply to those who in this dispensation had heard the Gospel and rejected it. We assured him most solemnly that no further opportunity would be given those who have heard the Gospel, and refused it, but that rather 2 Thes. ii. 10, 12, would be the result.

We visited a few of the women. Poor Susie Abbot had been confined to bed for a month, but is up again. She says, " I asked God to make me better, and He has done so"—she has a beautiful childlike mind. I am sure that Mr Campbell's kind, loving words to these dear people, will leave their mark on them.

17th May.—Mr Herbert Sims from Central Africa went to the Island to-day. Botha was the first we

A TERRIBLE SCOURGE

called upon. He had been very unwell but was recovering again, though still in bed. It is really touching to hear him speak of the goodness of God ; lifting his poor helpless hands, paralysed like his feet, he said, " My feet and my hands are paralysed, my eyes are blind, but then you must remember I have two ears to hear " (don't ask, what they are like), " and I have a mouth to speak, that's (hush) more than many have." Can you conceive such gratitude ? In leaving him, we were followed by a shower of " God bless you, God bless you, thank you, thank you, for coming to see me."

We saw Lucas, who seems very happy, and confident in the hope of our Lord's speedy return. " Oh, will it not be wonderful," said he, " when we go to be with the Lord ? " We spoke a little about the glorified body we shall have at His coming. The same poor leprous body will then be "transformed into a body of glory like unto His " (Phil. iii. 21). In No. 10, we had a word with Mr T., then saw poor Smith, who was very weak in bed. This man is English born, he is one of the only two English patients now on the Island. We had a very solemn word with him about his soul. He wept, as Mr Sims spoke to him and was evidently under deep conviction, but something seems to hinder his acceptance of Christ, and I cannot find out what it is. In such cases one sees the need of being able to follow them up. Mr Sims spoke to a few Kaffirs. As we look at the appalling needs of this Island, we are reminded of the words of a great man who once figured largely in this Colony, the late Cecil Rhodes, " Much to do, but little done."

ROBBEN ISLAND

2nd June.—Here I am, once more surrounded with misery and suffering, reminding one of the terrible Fall of man, through which it has all been brought about. Thank God, we know that if all this ruin and misery have been brought upon the human race through the fall of man, the death and resurrection of Christ has procured for all who trust in Him, immeasurable blessing. If we are to accept the common belief that leprosy is a type of sin, which no doubt it is, and if to human nature the thing itself is so repellent, how must sin appear in the sight of a Holy God! The words of the wise are in great evidence to-day, " Fools, make a mock of sin."

CHAPTER XVI.

VISITS TO THE TRANSVAAL.

2nd September.—For the past two months' I have been about in the Transvaal. During my visit there, I had rather an interesting experience at Pretoria. It happened in the following manner. I was staying with a brother in the Lord in Germiston. One day his wife asked, if I intended going to Pretoria. I replied, " No, I have no leading that way." She remarked that " The Christians there would be disappointed and perhaps stumbled if I did not go." I told her that I did not wish to disappoint them, and that I would write offering my services for a week-end. This I did, and received a reply immediately, which reached me when I was in Brakpan, saying that " they had arranged a service for the following Friday, and were making it known." What else could I do, but yield, in spite of an engagement at Johannesburg for the same evening.

On my arrival at Pretoria I was told that a meeting had been convened in Mr Hughes' large dining-room, and that night by seven o'clock it was packed, about fifty being present. My intention was to have spoken to Christians, but God would have it otherwise. One or two purely Gospel hymns were given out by some one present, which so deeply exercised my heart that I had to say with Peter of old, " What or who was I, that I could withstand God " (Acts xi. 17).

ROBBEN ISLAND

Praise God! no sooner did I yield, than my tongue was loosed and I spoke with much freedom.

At the close a brother asked if I was prepared for a Service on the Saturday. I replied, "You can arrange as many Services as you like, for me." One or two were spoken to as they passed out. On the Saturday evening a large motor bus was engaged to convey us to a sister's house in the country, where again I was determined to address Christians; but the Holy Spirit hindered me, and hymn after hymn, purely Gospel, was sung at the commencement. Once more, as I yielded, the Holy Spirit supplied the message—*Justified by Grace; Justified by Faith; Justified by Blood* (Rom. iii. 24, and v. 9).

At the close of the Service I spoke to one or two; it was then evident to me that the Holy Spirit was working mightily, one after another breaking down and weeping. Several professed to be saved that evening, and from that moment on, for days, there was such a working out of the Holy Spirit, as I had never seen before.

It would occupy too much space to give all the details of those few days' experience. Sufficient to say, I heard on my return to Johannesburg, that no less than twenty precious souls had passed out of death into life during that visit.

The evening before I left Pretoria, a goodly number came together in Mr Hughes' house, and I had the privilege of addressing them once more for about two hours.

At the close, a parting cup of tea was provided, and we continued talking until a late hour. During

VISITS TO THE TRANSVAAL

the conversation, the secret of all this blessing was revealed. It appears that several devoted sisters had agreed some months previously to wait upon God, and to ask Him "To send a servant of His to Pretoria, to preach the Gospel." At once, I understood the whole matter, and felt that it was only Acts xvi. 13, over again. The apostle was perplexed as to the way of the Lord, and as some one has said, "He did not know which way to go, so he retired to rest, little knowing that there were a few humble women praying by the river side."

CHAPTER XVII.

VISITORS TO THE ISLAND.

6th September.—Had the company of Mr Maitland, from Central Africa; he was cheered to see the work of grace, in many of these poor lepers on Robben Island.

I heard to-day that dear Susie Abbot fell asleep, about a month ago. What a happy release—she had been an inmate in the asylum for over twenty-four years. During all these years I have never on one single occasion heard a murmur from her lips. Few there are indeed, who are surrounded with earthly blessings, of whom this can be said.

Miss Gammon from Angola went over with me this week. I was not able to show her much of the work, as a good deal of our time was taken up in seeing some of the private patients.

However, I am sure our sister will be able to turn to good account what she saw and heard there.

September.—My brother and I were over. We could easily give the whole of our time to the Christians on the Island; they seem so eager to get some spiritual food, that they are quite prepared to allow their natural food to stand over. This is especially true of those who are blind. All this is very encouraging to us.

3rd November.—I had the privilege of taking Miss

VISITORS TO THE ISLAND

Walker to the Island; she is out here from Ireland on a short visit to her sister, Mrs Miller. She says, " One must visit the Island to get some idea of the condition of the people, and the work amongst them." I was able to show her a few of the worst cases, which deeply impressed her. For one who has never seen a leper, it is certainly very saddening to the heart. Nevertheless there is, for the trusting soul, a bright prospect looming up away in the future; for at His coming these bodies of theirs will most assuredly be changed, yea, even the poor leprous body; and then, as Miss Walker remarked, " we shall be worth looking at." I told Mr T. to-day that I had heard that Mr B., the Jewish Rabbi, had in his private class, advised his students to read the New Testament, adding, " it will assist you to a right understanding of the old." He seemed for a moment doubtful; however, he promised afterwards to read the New Testament. I sincerely hope that his eyes may be opened to see his need of Christ. I had prayer and a word with May de Ruck.

Had quite an encouraging time among the believers. We were noticing the great contrast between the sacrifices offered under the law, and the one great Sacrifice made, when Christ expired upon the Cross. The High Priest alone was allowed to enter the most Holy Place once a year. He could not take a single Israelite in with him, but, blessed be God, Christ has not only entered into heaven itself, of which the other was a type, but He leads the true worshipper in with Him. And then we have not only the privilege of entering into the " Holiest of Holies," but we are

ROBBEN ISLAND

invited to follow Him " without the camp " (Heb. xiii. 13). All this is new, and so stirring to those believers. One Christian told me of the life testimony of another, and said its effects were felt through the Island. I know that young man. One poor old coloured man (a little weak mentally) would insist upon it that I was his brother by some natural tie ! Of course, I allow him to enjoy the happy relationship ! I am thankful for the grace that makes us one in Christ.

December.—The late F. S. Arnot's eldest son went to the Island with me to-day, and like his dear father, he soon manifested a deep sympathy in those poor lepers. We were very glad to have him under our roof for a few days, before he left for Johannesburg. He seems exercised about going out into the mission field. Whilst on the Island to-day, we came in touch with Mr D., from Kimberley. He has only been there a few months, poor man ! His wife and family live in Kimberley. It was soon very evident that he was no friend to the Word of God. Oh, how helpless one feels in dealing with such men. For what can one do with a man who does not believe the Bible to be the Word of God ? The writings of almost any man of the world, in his opinion, were preferable to the Bible. I think he found himself in a tight corner once or twice. The following week a letter appeared in one of the local papers, in which reference was made to our conversation. This I trust is not a bad sign.

17th January 1921.—Mr and Mrs Marais, of Pretoria, accompanied me to-day. The sea was rather unpleasant, both going and returning, so that several

VISITORS TO THE ISLAND

were upset. My companions were very much impressed by their visit. We were able here and there, to deal with a few unsaved, and also to impart some words of cheer to God's suffering saints.

24th January.—I have had the pleasure of my friend, Mr Roeland's company, also of three Baptist ministers; namely, Messrs Maisey, Hopkins, and Lindsey. We first called at a few private rooms. Mr Roeland had a word with those who could understand a little English. It is wonderful to see how grateful poor Botha is, in spite of the sad condition of his body. I am sure these friends will never forget their first visit to Robben Island. We called for a few moments, on the man who had inserted a letter in one of the local papers. I told him that my attention had been drawn to it by a friend. He said that he was not referring to me, so I told him that I had no selfish motives in visiting him, but that it was his own welfare I had at heart. However, I am praying for him, that his heart may yet be softened.

Seeing a nice plate of food by the bedside of one poor fellow, I enquired, " Why do you not take your food ? " " Can't eat it, sir." It occured to me, if the Government could arrange to have a regular supply of fruit sent to the Island, such cases might now and then be given a little fruit, instead of the ordinary diet. However, I am afraid this is scarcely possible. What a boon it is to these poor lepers to get fruit. They often turn against their daily rations. How nice at such times to be able to stand by with a little fruit. But alas ! there are few tender hands and loving hearts to be found; for the poor leper's place,

ROBBEN ISLAND

is still "outside the camp." I mean outside the camp of most hearts. But "there was no room for the Saviour of sinners in the Inn." Nevertheless there is room in His heart for the poor leper. I am thankful to say, through the kindness of our dear friends in England and Ireland, who contribute so liberally of their substance for these poor creatures, that we are able to send them large quantities of fruit in the summer season.

March.—Mr Geddes, from Ireland (on his way to Central Africa), went with me to-day. I am sure from his remarks, that his visit will leave a deep and lasting impression upon him. After showing him round some of the wards, and speaking to one here and there, we settled down on the stoep of another ward, got a few of the women around us, and had a good time in speaking to them of God's love. The scene was very touching; nearly all were without hands or feet, and a few also blind. You ask, " Is there much pain with leprosy ? " No. Not very much keen physical pain, but think for a moment of the mental suffering and distress ! Imagine, if you can, how utterly helpless they are to do anything for themselves. I am sure it would have melted your heart, and brought tears to your eyes, to have heard those women singing some of their favourite Dutch hymns. Surely angels would fly to do the work entrusted now to sinners saved by Grace. May we value more highly our great privileges !

We dropped in and saw Botha for a moment. What an object of pity indeed ! Poor fellow ! he was very much touched, as we sang a couple of verses, in Dutch.

April.—Mrs Faithful, who is connected with the South African General Mission, went over with me

VISITORS TO THE ISLAND

to-day. She has long wished to visit the lepers, feeling that many are not able to intelligently sympathize with them, until they have seen them. She was most anxious to speak to the patients, but was hampered, by not knowing the Dutch language. We gathered a few of the females together in one of the wards, and held a Service. Mrs Faithful was much impressed with the eagerness of the women to listen.

27th May.—I was very much struck by the earnest testimony Botha gave this morning; it did my soul good to listen to him. He said there was a time when he was well and hearty on the mainland, but he was hardened in sin, and would not listen to the Word of God, although brought up under religious influence. But now, he justified God in afflicting him with this dire disease, in order to bring him to Himself. Said he, " When I had my eyesight I would not use it to read the Word of God. Now He has taken it from me." He believes that he will never cease in the Glory to praise God for lifting him out of the mire of sin, bringing him to Robben Island, and saving him there. He spoke of the boy who attends to him: " Look at that boy; he was once a drunkard, a dancer, and cared nothing for God or His Word, but now he has left it all." " Yes," said the boy, " it is all true what Botha says, and even after I was brought to the Island as a leper, I was not humbled until I saw what Grace had done for Botha, then I turned and accepted Christ as my Saviour." Small died a few days ago. A happy release for him. Had a nice word with May de Ruck; and others were present.

25th July.—Have not been able to get across for

ROBBEN ISLAND

several weeks; sometimes through stormy weather, other times too busy on the mainland. Had a pleasant and profitable talk with B.; he always appreciates my calls. In speaking of the return of our Lord, I felt the need of knowing more of the power of it in my own soul! How easy it is to have one's head filled with the doctrine, and at the same time know very little of the power in one's heart and life. In No. 1 Ward, I noticed two boys sitting by the bedside of one, whom I afterwards learned was their brother. On further investigation, I found that there were no less than seven belonging to one family on the Island, all lepers; mother, four sons, and two daughters; only one sister at home, father already dead. Truly leprosy is a loathsome disease! One needs a real heart of compassion, fired by the love of God to visit these poor outcast sufferers. A similar family at Murray's Bay, touched me deeply. A Mrs G., once a nice-looking woman—so humble and gentle—a true child of God is there, with all her family, *i.e.* four sons. The eldest is a fine young man of seventeen summers, who was in the seventh standard, when he was torn from school with his three brothers, and together with his mother brought to Robben Island. I had a little talk with them to-day, promising to have a longer conversation when I came again. How little one is able to accomplish in the few hours one has on the Island. The time is altogether too short to deal with so many. Oh, to be able to do what the poet says:

> "To meet the glad with joyful smiles
> And to wipe the weeping eyes;
> With a heart at leisure from itself,
> To soothe and sympathise."

VISITORS TO THE ISLAND

15th August.—Miss Gibson, sister of Mrs Mowat, here from Central Africa, went over with me to-day. The weather was not very pleasant, there being wind, rain, and rough sea; however, the rains kept off most of the time whilst we were on the Island, so that we were able to visit a few of the patients. We held a little Service for some of the coloured women, several of whom were blind, footless and handless. We had a word with Lucas, who is bright and full of hope touching the Lord's return. His life testimony is a power on the Island. Botha is a sad case; it is really painful to look upon his disfigured face. I do not suppose there is a sound spot in his body; his eyes are just covered with flies, which must be extremely trying. Oh, for a grateful heart to praise our God for preservation from the awful malady!

30th August.—I was wavering in my mind whether I would go over to-day or not, but I am thankful that I went, as the young man, Eccles, with whom I spoke a fortnight ago was very weak. I had a most earnest time with him, and urged upon him to close with God's offer of salvation without delay, and so far as I can judge he did so. One cannot be too thankful, if in any measure we are guided by the Lord; the tendency is to take our own way. However, it seems to me that it was of the Lord's special ordering that I went over to-day. For I am persuaded that that young man is nearing his end.

I had a profitable conversation with B. and Botha together, and later with Lucas. What a privilege to to be in the way to cheer some of God's dear banished ones on this Island!

ROBBEN ISLAND

1st September.—I had the pleasure of taking Dr Tilsley to the Island to-day. He arrived the day before from England, with Messrs Sharp and Elliot. Dr Tilsley had a long and interesting conversation with Dr Davis regarding leprosy, after which we visited some of the male patients, then went on to Murray's Bay and held a Service for the women, for which they appeared to be very grateful. God grant we may meet them all in the Glory. I know, poor things, that they long to be in that bright and blessed home, where sorrow, pain, nor sickness, can never come. But Oh, how difficult it is for many of them to apprehend the most simple truths. Dr Davis told me that the young man Eccles died yesterday, and others informed me that he fell asleep peacefully. How thankful I am that I went over on Monday.

27th September.—Was specially helped of the Lord to speak a word to Smith, but his mind seems as dark as midnight. Botha was very ill, but the peace of God fills his heart. Poor Albertyn, he is a similar case, stone blind, and full of open ulcers from head to foot. I spoke to him of his security in Christ. There is no wavering with him; his faith is firm. It was very rough on leaving the Island; the small boat at the jetty was now and then buried in the spray. I lost my hat overboard, but by making a quick dash I managed to get it again.

5th October.—I am writing on board the boat on our return journey. I was not able to meet with many of the patients to-day; I remained too long with a few in the private rooms. This makes me long more and more to settle on the Island, at least for a time (six

VISITORS TO THE ISLAND

months or a year), but whether I shall obtain permission from the Government or not, is a question. However, I purpose trying my best. My dear brother and I have cast the net for many a day, and now we want to draw it in, hence, in my opinion, one needs to be on the spot to follow up the work daily. We have just laid to rest my dear wife's aunt—in her ninetieth year—whom we had under our care for seventeen years, so that we are now quite free to go to the Island, subject to the will of God.

October.—I wrote to the Commissioner requesting his permission to be allowed to stay on the Island. A week later I had a private interview with him in his own office, where he received me very kindly, and expressed his great appreciation of our work for these many years. But he added that he regretted he was unable to concede to my request, as it would create a precedent that was most undesirable. Of course I understood what he meant. He advised my seeing Dr Davis, and hearing what he had to say, as he valued the doctor's judgment in such matters. I called and saw Dr Davis, who promised to do what he could in the matter, but I have heard nothing further, and have now given up all hope of being allowed to go there to permanently stay.

A special Gospel Campaign, by Messrs Elliot and Sharp, has occupied a good deal of my time of late. It has been a wonderful time of blessing, souls seeking the Lord almost every night. Mr Elliot is no doubt an able preacher of the Gospel and a real soul-winner. Every one may not fall in fully with the lines upon which he works, but we shall become the better helpers by praying for him, rather than finding fault.

12th December.—I was favoured with the company of Messrs Elliot and Sharp to-day, and was glad to find Mr Otto, the Superintendent of the male lepers, on board, so that I could arrange with him for a Service for the men in the morning, and one for the women in the afternoon. We had short meetings here and there, and I showed them as much of the work as I could, in the limited time at our disposal.

I was impressed with a sight that I shall not soon forget; four native women huddled together in a little tin hut, about five feet square, their poor bodies mutilated by that terrible disease. I beckoned Messrs Elliot and Sharp to come near, but at once the poor things shrank back with shame and protested against it, and although I assured them of our fullest sympathy they still drew back. It struck me that after all, deeper than the black skin, there was clearly manifested the delicate feelings which belongs to woman. My companions were interested in watching a woman kneeling before a tub and washing clothes, although she was without hands, having just the two stumps!

6th January 1922.—This morning, when about half way over, the engine broke down which caused some delay. My brother was on board, and in one way I was sorry, for he has not been well for weeks past, and that it did him no good. There was a strong south-east wind blowing at the time, so we drifted before it. It has been very warm also, which made it trying to get round. However, I hope we were able to cheer a few sad hearts. What a blessed release it

VISITORS TO THE ISLAND

will be for many of them when they are taken home, either through the grave, or at our Lord's coming, This is the one great inspiring hope and comfort that these sufferers have.

13th January.—Two have died since we were last over; one whom I tried to see last week, but was unable so to do. I heard to-day that he passed away, resting on the finished work of Christ. I wish I could have had another word with him before he went home. The other man, Small, I have every reason to believe has gone to be with the Lord.

Lucas is growing brighter and brighter; it can truly be said of him, " Though the outward man perish, yet the inward man is renewed day by day." He still bears a good testimony on the Island, and to him the return of the Lord is a growing reality. Botha still lingers and keeps bright.

23rd January.—I questioned one who is blind, as to whether he would be able to see again. " Oh, yes," he replied, "not now, but at the Lord's coming."

The face of one very bright believer in No. 3 Ward literally beamed with joy as we opened up the Word of God ; indeed, he actually laughed for very joy of heart.

My thoughts have been much occupied to-day with the work of the Holy Spirit, first, in preparing the soil, casting in the good seed, watering it, watching it's growth, and reaping the fruit. Isa. xxviii. 23 to end ; 2 Tim. ii. 6 7, " The husbandman must first be partaker of the fruits." Others look on and " glorify God in us."

1st March.—Have been greatly helped in speaking

ROBBEN ISLAND

to the patients. One of those experiences, alas, not too common, when you realise that your words are gripping your hearers. Oh, to be more passive in His hands, that He may mould and fashion us more perfectly for His service. After dealing at length with a little batch of men, at least one was, I believe, led to Christ. It is astonishing how utterly dull some are regarding spiritual things, yet on the other hand, there are those who are bright and intelligent. So we feel the need of the Word continually. " Be not weary in well doing, for ye shall reap in due time, if ye faint not."

8th March.—I did not feel very bright when leaving for the Island to-day; but I was enabled by His grace to do a little for the patients. I had nothing to eat until just before leaving. Some of the lepers who are anxious that I should settle there for a time, thought that I ought to write to the Commissioner once more. They told me that they had spoken to the Superintendent, and he also thought I should speak to the Commissioner again. Personally, I am not very clear about it, though most anxious to obtain his permission; I can truly say " Thy will be done."

15th March.—I was disappointed on reaching the Docks this morning, to find that the boat was not going over, it being too rough to land, so I did not go this week. My brother, however, went over the next day with a small party, to give the patients a special treat. They remained there for a few days.

29th March.—Two young sisters in the Lord, Miss Doris Lee and Miss Hilda Beaumont, accompanied

VISITORS TO THE ISLAND

me to-day. I was able to show them a little of the work, and I trust their visit will bear fruit in the future. There is nothing like a personal visit to let Christians clearly understand the nature of the work.

3rd April.—Mr Combs, from Durban, visited with me, and I was thankful for his fellowship. After seeing a few of the private patients, and passing through two or three of the wards, speaking to some, confined to their beds, we took the trolly at 1 p.m., for Murray's Bay. I spoke for some time with a young girl who has been there only for a year. I believe she was enabled to see the truth of the Gospel more clearly. I hope to help her further on my next visit. We were just about leaving for the boat, when a very dear Christian woman, who has not been there very long, was anxious to bring some of the blind women together for a little Service; we had very little time, but they were so anxious for it, that it was hard to refuse. They were quickly brought together, and we commenced with hymn 83, " God only light, before whose face " (in Dutch). Poor things ! They listened most eagerly to the story of the Cross, but I found by the time we had finished, that we only had twenty minutes to catch the boat—half an hour's walk—however, we ran and walked, not an uncommon experience for some of us ; fortunately when about half way back we met a trolly ; the man at once turned round and kindly brought us back, otherwise we might have lost the boat. It reminds me of an experience I had years ago, when I did lose it, and had to remain on the Island for two days ; that same evening after tea, I went back to the wards, but on my way

ROBBEN ISLAND

down I called at a private room, where two brothers were living. There I met a young man for the first time, who had only been a week on the Island. That very night God saved him, and he became very bright. He was from a very good family, his father being a large contractor.

15th May.—Mr Dubbeldam went over with me for a few days, for special meetings among the lepers. We held small Services in the wards throughout the day, finishing up each evening with a good Gospel lantern Service in a large building provided for that purpose. It was deeply touching to see from two to three hundred lepers assembled together to hear the Gospel in their own mother tongue. Mr Dubbeldam, being a Hollander, speaks Dutch well. What a sight! To witness numbers of them, handless, footless, and some blind, crawling and hobbling along as best they could, to hear the good news! Four professed to be saved, during this special effort.

12th June.—Was round my old parish to-day. Had a little talk with those who professed during my visit with Mr Dubbeldam. One seemed very clear and happy; the others will need a little more help. It is exceedingly difficult for some to grasp the most elementary truths of the Gospel, so long have they been accustomed to "other Gospels."

I spoke to a bright believer confined to bed in No. 1. At times he laughed aloud for joy, as I spoke to him of the glorious future that awaited him at the coming of the Lord. We had taught him some verses to sing during our stay there; now he is continually singing them, sometimes in the night season, " Ever-

VISITORS TO THE ISLAND

lasting life is free," " I am included," etc. On returning to the boat I called at a private room, where I saw a dear fellow; his bodily condition is dreadful in the extreme; open running sores, his face is terrible to behold, mouth and lips all open sores, too awful to describe. I sat a little distance from him, for it is almost impossible to come very near such cases: What could one say? I told him I felt dumb, for the very best comfort that I could offer was poor and mean, when compared with the comfort of God. I urged upon him to try and keep his eyes upon the quickly coming One, for He may come ere I leave the Island, then that poor torn body will be changed and fashioned like unto His body of glory. Poor fellow! It seemed too much and too grand for his faith to grasp.

21st June.—Worked among the men in the morning, and went to Murray's Bay in the afternoon. A good many of the women were up at the men's wards celebrating some one's birthday. Poor things they are glad of anything, to break the monotony.

28th *June.*—I was speaking to a little girl to-day, Dorothy de Waal. She is about fifteen years old. Her stepfather told me one day that he had spent £1000, on doctors, before she was brought to the Island, in order to obtain a cure. I am inclined to question the truth of this statement. I said to the little girl, " Where is your home, Dorothy ? " " In Cape Town, sir," was her reply. " Do you know of another home ? " I asked. " Yes, heaven, sir." " Which would be the easier to get to, Dorothy ? " To my surprise the dear girl declared, " Heaven."

ROBBEN ISLAND

I then went on to tell her that it would not be easy to leave the Island, and return to her earthly home. She would first need to be cured of her leprosy; and doctors at present know of no cure. And then she would need a Government discharge; likewise, neither could she go to heaven until first cleansed from her sins. I told her all that was possible, since Jesus had died. She is fairly intelligent; but as to the body, I am afraid her case is hopeless.

10th July.—I was not able to go over last week, the boat having gone on the slip for cleaning. I was doubtful about getting there even this morning, as there was a very heavy fog when I left Wynberg. However, on reaching the Docks I found it was not so bad. I spoke very earnestly to Mr Y., who is badly afflicted, and confined to bed. I am afraid he does not yet know the Lord, as I thought. I spoke also to a nice young girl, also confined to her bed, but Oh, the density of the mind! However, I trust she was helped a little. Mrs G. is up again. As far as I can judge, she is a Christian, but what a heavy cross to be there with her four fine sons, all hopelessly afflicted! Our engine broke down again, soon after leaving the Island.

12th July.—Mr J. B. was anxious that I should see Mr Y. to-day, as he was very ill, but would have nothing to do with him, nor any one else who came to speak to him with reference to his soul; so I went in fear and trembling, Mr B. promising to pray for me. I called at his room which was near by, and all I can say is, that in the first stage he just suffered me to speak to him. I pleaded with him most earnestly. After a

VISITORS TO THE ISLAND

little prayer, and before leaving, he assured me that he was trusting in the finished work of Christ.

17th July. There was a thick fog in going over to-day. One always feels glad when the Island is sighted. Saw B. again, then called at Mr Y's. room. The dear man is now rejoicing in the Lord. Several of the Christians came together and sang Dutch hymns with him. His poor wife was in the room to-day—had just come over for two days. What a pathetic sight! The husband lying in bed sorely afflicted, and at a table a little distance away, his wife sitting weeping—a fine respectable lady. It is really surprising how this disease finds its way into such families.

Went over to Murray's Bay and had a splendid time with some of the women. Spoke from Acts iii. *re* the crippled man; noticed four things concerning him—he was helpless, he was poor, he was outside, and he was hopeless. I had the conviction in my soul, that the Holy Spirit was carrying home the Word. I also had an earnest word with two young men in No. 1.

CHAPTER XVIII.

"FAITH HEALERS" AT ROBBEN ISLAND.

22nd July.—Mr Hickson, the gentleman who believes in "Faith Healing," the Bishop and a few other ministers, made a special visit to the Island to-day, for the purpose of dealing with the leper patients, with a view, if possible, to the healing of their disease. I had heard of this projected visit, and felt, at least, that it was my duty to go over and watch the proceedings.

We left the docks at 9 a.m., and the Island at 4.30 p.m., so that we had an extra long day.

The first Service was held in the English Church building, where about two hundred male lepers were assembled. Mr Hickson addressed the patients in a very quiet sympathetic manner, evidently impressed by such a touching sight.

He said that he could not think that God wished them to be continually suffering in the manner they were. He wished them to have healthy bodies, and that he had come to the Island to encourage them to pray to God for their recovery. He said, " You must not look to me; I have no power to heal you; no man has; God only can do that. I shall lay my hands upon you in the Name of Jesus Christ, and pray over you.

"FAITH HEALERS" AT ROBBEN ISLAND

If healing does not come immediately, don't be discouraged, go on praying. In my experience most cases of healing have been gradual. If you have sin on your conscience, confess it to God. But you have a deeper need than the healing of your body—the healing of your soul, and even if your body is healed, and not your soul, then in the sight of God you are not healed at all." This was the sum and substance of his address.

It was most impressive to witness 200 poor afflicted people hobbling and crawling to the Church to have his hands laid upon them, no doubt full of hope and expectation that healing would come their way immediately. Two Services for the women were afterwards held at Murray's Bay, which I also attended. A number who were confined to bed were also visited, Mr Y. among the number.

I held a short conversation with Mr Hickson on our return from the Island. As far as I can judge, he is sincere in what he believes to be the mind of God, but that may be said of some who are clearly off God's lines of truth. Mr Hickson uses expressions at times which many of us could not use. However, I was glad to hear him say in course of conversation, that Christ was more to him than anything else.

The boat did not go over on the following Monday, consequently I could not get over before Wednesday, when I learned that Mr Y. had taken a turn for the worse on Sunday, the very next day after Mr Hickson had laid his hands on him. The doctor telegraphed for his wife on the Monday, and she, and two of the family, went over on the Tuesday in a motor boat.

ROBBEN ISLAND

I found him very weak in bed. Read part of 2 Cor. v., to him, reminding him of the glorified body that awaited him at the coming of the Lord; he seemed comforted, though almost too weak to speak. He was covered up so that his face could not be seen, even by his poor sorrowing wife, who was sitting at a small table some distance from the bed, weeping. On the stoep was a son, a fine young man, and in the room was a young daughter. I placed my hand upon her shoulder, reminding her that her dear father would soon be with the Lord, and if she wished to meet him there, she would have to go by the same way, namely, " By way of the Cross." Poor girl, amidst tears and sobs, she declared that she had accepted Christ as her Saviour.

8th August.—It was too stormy to get to the Island last week, but have been over to-day, though we received a 'phone message from the Island telling us not to leave before 10.45, as it was too rough to land. Of course this makes our time very limited. I learnt on arrival this morning, that Mr Y. had passed away last week, full of confidence and happy in the Lord. He was conscious up to the last. He told his wife, that he did not want to remain here, and that he knew that he was going to be with the Lord, and that Mr Fish had made things so clear to him. He gave his wife instructions regarding his home, also counselling his son, a fine young man still at College, to care for his mother. I do thank God, for this wonderful trophy of His abounding grace, practically saved at the eleventh hour. Who are we that we should be so used of God?

"FAITH HEALERS" AT ROBBEN ISLAND

Lukas told me to-day of some striking verses which he asked them to sing, just before he fell asleep. Only a short time back he would have nothing to do with any of them. Had a nice time with Lukas; we both prayed before I left him. His poor blind eyes were filled with tears.

28th August.—Stormy weather has prevented me getting over for the past two weeks. To-day, however, we were able to go across, my brother going to Murray's Bay, I remaining with the male patients. In J. B's. room I met the second youngest son of Mrs G., and had another solemn talk with him regarding his soul. Spoke to several in No. 1. Before leaving, I called and saw Albertyn. One of the attendants was present, dressing his wounds, so I waited until he had finished. And I must confess, that I had to muster all my nerve and courage to remain. It is no exaggeration to say that this poor creature is the identical case of Isa. i. 6; but one must be present and see such cases with the bandages off, to fully realise their awfulness. After the attendant had finished I spoke to him from Rom. viii. 18 to end. He is blind, and bandaged from head to foot and speaks by means of a silver tube in his windpipe. I thought of the words of the prophet when the question was put to him, "Son of man, can these bones live? O Lord God, Thou knowest." And so to my question, "Can this body be changed and fashioned like unto The body of Christ's Glory," comes the answer, "He is able to subdue all things unto Himself" (Phil. iii. 21).

8th September.—Mr Fellingham, from Natal, who is here to meet his fiancee, Miss Diver, from England,

ROBBEN ISLAND

went over to-day with my brother, his wife, and myself. We called on a few of the private patients, and found Mr B. very ill. I read to him, 1st Peter i., and had a little prayer, and he seemed comforted. Poor Albertyn is unable to sleep at nights, he can never lie down. Mr Fellingham spoke to a Kaffir in No. 1. We prayed by his bedside, and the poor fellow wept. Mr Fellingham seems to have made fair progress in the language.

I was asked to call and see a youth who is very weak in bed—Willie Boezag. I was surprised to find that he is a son of old Mr Boezag, who was a bright shining star for God on the Island, a wonderful trophy of grace—now long since with the Lord. I was glad indeed to find his son also trusting in the Lord.

13th September.—I had the pleasure to-day of taking Mr and Mrs Coleridge over, also Mr Light. They had just arrived from home, to labour for the Lord in the Transvaal. We first called on some of the private patients, and later went to Murray's Bay, where we had two good meetings for the women. Our friends were, of course, at a loss to some extent, not being acquainted with the Dutch language. I spoke from John i, " Christ, the light of the world," and explained that the darkness of the human heart is more dense than the darkness of Egypt—a darkness which could be felt ; reminding them that they were responsible for the opening of their hearts to allow Him to enter who is the True Light. I used the illustration of a lighted lamp brought into a dark room ; at once the darkness is dispelled, and this was an example of our responsibility in allowing our lights

"FAITH HEALERS" AT ROBBEN ISLAND

to shine that others may see them. We then sang a few Dutch hymns.

18th September.—J. B. is still in bed, and is under the impression that he will not get up again. Willie Boezag is also still very weak. The time soon passes in calling upon one and another. I have had a poisoned finger for the past six weeks, and for a time had rather grave fears that I might have come in too close contact with the disease. The doctor resident on the Island is fully convinced that it is contagious but assures me that I have no need to fear with regard to my finger. Oh, for a heart to praise my God, not only because from sin set free, but from leprosy preserved.

25th September.—Visited Albertyn to-day. He says, " I am not afraid to die, Mr Fish ; I know when the Lord takes me, I shall go to heaven ; He will not let me be lost." It is wonderful to see the simplicity of faith in this poor blind patient ; he is not able to lie down either by day or night, for fear of suffocation, and he can only speak as he puts his fingers on the tube in his windpipe.

I was struck on hearing a Xosa boy say to-day ; " Jesus wanted to save me, therefore He came and died for me." It was the manner in which he put it—in his own language—that arrested my attention. I met with another very intelligent old native to-day. He was reading from John vi. He said, " Christ, the Living Bread, is not like the bread that Moses gave the people, for they ate of that bread and died. If we eat of the Living Bread we shall never die." He was wonderfully clear on the subject, and I really received help from the old man. He afterwards referred to the two witnesses, the Spirit Within and the Word Without, and how beautifully they agree; a twofold witness that we belong to God. I asked him if he loved to read God's Word, " Oh, yes," he replied, " I could not get along without that."

We brought back a young girl to-day, who has been on the Island for many years; and this is the third time that she has been released. Both her feet are gone, but they have managed to give her artificial feet; both hands are badly affected. I felt deeply for the poor girl; she is really a beautiful looking girl. I am afraid she does not yet know the Lord, though she has heard the Gospel hundreds of times from our lips. She was a Roman Catholic, but gave that up more than a year ago; and has since been attending little meetings they have for prayer, just among themselves. After she recovered from sea-sickness I went to her and had what I said might be, " my last word with you." I said, " If after all, you are led to accept Christ as your Saviour, as a result of what you have heard of Him on that Island, then you will have to thank God, notwithstanding your sore affliction, that you were ever confined there; and I shall rejoice to meet you in heaven. But all the praise, honour, and glory will be due to Him Who died to bring you there."

2nd October.—Have not been able to go over for some days. It has been too stormy, with a heavy sea running. Now I am glad of the opportunity, and have been kept busy all day.

8th November.—Just before entering the wards, I bowed my head before God, asking Him to guide

"FAITH HEALERS" AT ROBBEN ISLAND

me to such as would be willing to listen to His Word; and I am sure He heard my prayer, so that I was able to deal with a good number. I met with one man who was specially interested, and fairly intelligent. After reading some portions regarding his lost condition, and God's perfect remedy, he said, "I see it now, sir." It was interesting to notice the immediate change which came over his face. Truly the words of the Psalmist come in here, "The entrance of Thy words giveth light; it giveth understanding to the simple." Jeremiah says, "Thy Words were found, and I did eat them, and Thy Word was unto me the joy and rejoicing of my heart." Before I left him he said, "I hope when you come again, sir, that I shall be able to give you a clear testimony as to my faith in Jesus Christ."

17th November.—The weather was rather unpleasant, in fact, the captain had us all on the bridge, coming back, as the sea was washing on board. Found Lucas and Albertyn still very bright. Called again at No. 3, in the afternoon, but did not see the man who professed to be saved the previous week.

I spoke to another man who told me that there was a time in his life when he trembled at the very thought of death, but now he had no fear whatever of dying. It is encouraging to get such a testimony, for as a rule these people are led to believe from their childhood that there is no such thing as the assurance of salvation on this side of the grave.

27th November.—The last few verses of Luke xxiv. were very much before me all day. To my mind the whole scene is so different from what one might

ROBBEN ISLAND

naturally expect. Our blessed Lord had gained the affections of His few followers so thoroughly, that one might reasonably expect to find them broken down, and full of sorrow, instead of which we find them rejoicing; " They worshipped Him, and returned to Jerusalem with great joy." If the scene of departure be such a happy one, what will the meeting be? He had told them previously, more than once, that He was about to leave them, but that He would come again (John xiv. 16); and now He would have their hearts occupied with His coming, and not with His going.

CHAPTER XIX.

ONE SOWETH, ANOTHER REAPETH.

11th December.—I had the pleasure of taking Mr Hugh Morrison with me. This was his first visit, and I am sure he will not soon forget it, neither will he fail to put it to good account. He was greatly surprised to see the extent of the work, and how little we were able to do in the limited time allowed. He felt humbled before God, as he listened to the bright testimony of some, to whom the coming of the Lord was a stirring reality. After all, the poor leper has little more in this world to cheer his heart; he has no prospects in this life, and even if he ever had, they are now like an egg dashed to the ground. He has no hope either, for as yet no cure has been discovered for his terrible malady. In one sense, he is worse off than the leper of old, for then the High Priest had the authority to pronounce him clean, but there is no earthly priest to do that now. Thank God, for the honour conferred on some of us, to be allowed to proclaim healing for the soul in the Name of the Lord, which is infinitely more important. I have been able to speak very earnestly to some, and I cannot think that God will allow His Holy Word to fall to the ground. One dear fellow was enabled, as far as I could judge, to lay hold on Christ. I learned afterwards, that a bright believer in the same ward, had

ROBBEN ISLAND

spoken to him the previous day; thus the saying was true, " One soweth and another reapeth " (John iv. 37).

20th Jauuary 1928.—I have not been able to visit the Island much of late, having had the responsibility of the Gospel Tent, at Wellington, where meetings were held, by Mr H. A. Voke, late of Swansea, for five weeks with good results, several being saved. I am glad to know that my brother keeps up regular visits to the patients, in spite of wind or sea. We were over together, to-day. Poor Albertyn is nearing his end. He is one of the most awful sights human eyes can behold. There were two patients sitting near him, driving off the swarms of flies that were feeding upon his terrible ulcers. He tried to speak, as I read to him 2 Cor. v., but he was too weak. I am satisfied that this day, some were helped for eternity.

A few days ago I called at the Old Somerset Hospital, to see a native boy from Central Africa, called Polo. He is Mr Clarke's boy, and was there for examination as a leper, just waiting then for his transfer to Robben Island. He is a nice Christian lad, about seventeen years of age, and very useful to Mr Clarke for translation work.

21st January.—Dear Albertyn obtained his release to-day.

31st January.—I was not able to go over on Monday, as the boat left half an hour early. Several were left behind. However, I managed it to-day, and saw a few of the patients, mostly believers. I met with two very sad cases in No.1. Their faces were awfully disfigured; it was almost impossible to sit near enough to them to speak to them. One had his face covered

ONE SOWETH, ANOTHER REAPETH

all over with white wadding, only holes cut for the mouth and eyes. Again the question comes before me, "Lord, how can this body be changed into a glorious body like unto Thine?" And I have to bow before Him, with Whom nothing is impossible, and say once more, "Thou art able to subdue all things unto Thyself" (Phil. iii. 21).

20th February.—The Superintendent was on board this morning. In course of conversation, he told me that in all probability, in the near future all the leper patients would be removed to the mainland, and distributed among the different leper Institutes. There are only 385 patients on the Island at the present time; whereas for many years there were about 680 to 700. One wonders what the Government intends doing with the Island. There is some talk about converting it into a big wireless station. If that be the case, then our work among the lepers—so far as the Island is concerned—will be brought to a close. However, we can thank God for all the years of good service, and for many who have found a refuge in Christ, through our ministry. It was a great pleasure to tell again to-day, of God's redeeming love. It is blessed to watch the earnest manner in which some drink in the Word; and although it is difficult for many of them to grasp the most simple truths, yet here and there one sees the effect of His Word produced, in a real change of life; but for the full harvest we must patiently wait. "The Word that goeth forth out of my mouth shall not return unto me void" (Dutch, *empty*).

2nd March.—J. B. is still in bed. I read a portion

of the Word to him. He was very grateful for the visit.

I saw Dr Davis about Polo. He says that he is a decided leper, but the Government is considering his application to be allowed to go back to the Congo again; he thinks there will be no objection to his return.

Botha and Lucas are fairly well. I had a nice talk with the latter; he is always ready for the Word, and it is difficult to satisfy his hungry soul.

I heard to-day that the Government has decided to send away from the the Island, 136 patients. Some, I understand, are being sent back to their own homes; and it has been said that by next year, all the patients will be away to the mainland. This remains to be seen; I am rather doubtful about it myself.

25th March.—I was accompanied to-day by my dear wife and two young sisters. We visited a few of the male patients, and afterwards went down to Murray's Bay. The women were very pleased to see my wife again, especially as she was able to speak to them freely in Dutch. They pressed her to come again soon. She had not been able to go over for many years. There are a few distressing cases on the island just now; the condition of some of their poor bodies, is indescribable. If we are to consider leprosy as a type of sin, then it reveals the old carnal nature as utterly corrupt. The very word "leper," strange enough, is sufficient to repel one from approaching them; and does not the very word *sin*, make a sincere child of God shrink back also with horror? How much more so, a Holy God?

12th March.—Had a good long talk with Polo.

ONE SOWETH, ANOTHER REAPETH

He says that I have shown him things in the Bible, that he had never seen before. Coming back I also had an interesting conversation with Mr Louw, the Dutch Reformed minister. I believe him to be a very sincere Christian, who together with his wife, is seeking earnestly the welfare of the patients.

18*th April.*—If I had pleased myself this morning, I should not have gone over, for I felt anything but well; however we are not here to please ourselves. My dear wife did not feel happy about my going either; still I knew I could count upon her prayers; and better still, His Word, " Certainly I will be with thee." The boat rolled a good bit, which did not improve matters. I called at Koning's room first, as I had a parcel for him from my brother. The poor fellow is very weak and is suffering much. His brother from Port Elizabeth, went over to-day, and will, I suppose, remain there for some days.

I spoke to several in No. 1 Ward. One man, whose daughter was sitting by his bedside, has been on the Island for twenty-seven years. He appears to be trusting in the Lord. His daughter was moved to tears, as I spoke to her about her soul. Had an interesting conversation with Polo on 1st and 2nd chapters of Phil. Oh, for grace to understand and appreciate more fully, the deep mysterious humiliation of the Son of God, that most glorious Person!

16*th April.*—There was a real old-fashioned southeaster to-day, and we got a little wet at the jetty. Mrs Henderson, from Natal, on the s.s. *Berrima*, was to have gone over with me, but on account of the strong wind, the boat could not dock.

ROBBEN ISLAND

I found poor Koning very weak and suffering intense agony; his brother, from Port Elizabeth, was with him, also one of the female patients. His brother removed the sheet that I might see the condition of his body, and I shall never forget the sight. I could only humbly thank God, for preserving me from such an awful affliction. I was not quite sure if Koning was saved, and scarcely knew what to read to him. But after reading several portions calculated to strip him of all self-confidence, he assured me that he was resting on the finished work of Christ. The poor fellow was very faint, and after 'phoning to the stores for some eau-de-Cologne, I left him with a word of prayer. A few people under a tree, afforded the opportunity for a real plain word; the Lord grant that it may bear fruit.

25th April.—We were tossed about considerably in crossing, and the boatman said that "The sea was coming up like wildfire." Orders were given for the passengers to be on the jetty at 12.45, as the boat must leave at 1 o'clock, which of course, meant that very little would be done to-day. On returning to the jetty, I found that the sea had risen very considerably, and the breakers were reaching far in towards the mainland. The Commissioner came along, and suggested my remaining over until the next day. I was afraid my wife would be anxious about me, and although he offered to telephone to her, I thanked him, but said I had better return. The boat certainly made a few nasty lurches, but, on the whole, she behaved fairly well. " He knows, H. knows, and tempers every wind that blows."

Two women, both without feet, blind, and one minus hands. The man standing, an earnest Christian whom God is using.

Taken by Messrs Sharp and Elliot, who went with me to the Island. The patient is seen holding his finger on a silver tube inserted into his windpipe. He is a nice believer.

ONE SOWETH, ANOTHER REAPETH

4th May.—Messrs Logan and Horton, on their way to the interior, went over to-day. As usual, we called at a few private rooms, then passed through some of the wards. Later on, we visited the females, where I had already arranged for a Service. It was encouraging to see a nice number listening to the story of the Cross ; our young brethren will not soon forget their visit here to the lepers.

25th May.—The sisters of the Cape Town Assembly, knitted sixteen woollen scarves, and my sister-in-law and I, distributed them among the men, who were very pleased to get them now in this cold weather. It is a real pleasure to give them anything; they are so grateful. One man sent for me to tell me that God had spoken to him through a book which had been given him. I had a talk with him, and he appears to be in earnest about his soul. I hope to see him the next time I go over, and have a longer conversation with him.

Called at the leper lunatic asylum, where there were twelve men ; John Jacobs, a criminal, was confined in an enclosure by himself ; he was quite rational as we spoke to him. I had not seen him for years, and concluded he was dead, but he knew me at once, and commenced speaking about the Lord. We had a most interesting time with the man, and were really astonished at his intelligent answers in the things of God.

29th May.—It was very calm this morning, the only unpleasant thing being a thick fog. I had a further conversation with Mr M. respecting the condition of the departed saints, a matter he was not very clear about last week. He understood that the words, "clothed upon," in 2nd Cor. v., meant that the believer would have a body immediately after leaving this world, and now the question was what kind of body would he have? We dealt with the subject very fully, and at the close he seemed clearer on the matter, remarking " that he had received quite a lift heavenward."

Lukas told me that he had asked to be transferred to the Pretoria leper asylum, on account of his weak chest. His deep regret was, that he would miss our visits, adding, " The only thing I care to live for is, the glory of God." He said, " God had been showing me my nothingness of late, and I am satisfied that there is nothing good in me naturally." This is surely the way to grow upward, by self-abnegation, low thoughts of self.

I had a very serious talk with the man whom I spoke to last week; he is an intelligent man, and as far as I can judge, sincere, but not yet fully able to grasp the full truth of the Gospel.

4th June.—It was very cold crossing this morning. I was on the bridge with the captain, and got a little shelter from the wind behind the canvas screen.

Had an earnest word with Polo, with regard to his life testimony on the Island.

25th June.—Mr and Mrs Hopkins, of China, accompanied me, and although they have met with lepers in that land, I question if they ever saw such cases as they found on Robben Island. We held several short Services, mostly in Dutch, so few understand English; I am sure God spoke to some. In

ONE SOWETH, ANOTHER REAPETH

speaking to a few women outside one of the huts, Mr Hopkins produced a small chart in Chinese characters; " The Upward and Downward Roads," which we were able to turn to good account, by explaining it to them in Dutch.

We were speaking to a young girl confined to bed, and had it not been in a female ward I would have taken her to be a man from forty to fifty years of age; such a face is absolutely indescribable; her mouth wide open, gasping for breath!

Beatrice, a young girl in the next bed was, I believe, definitely led to Christ. We knelt at her bedside, whilst Mr and Mrs Hopkins commended her to the Lord in prayer. Another poor soul, no hands or feet, said, " Oh, I have been longing to see you." But we had to leave her, for want of time.

4th July.—Two missionaries from Rhodesia, Misses Riphagen and Krige, went over this morning. The former is a highly trained nurse, anxious to get all the information she can regarding the best treatment for leprosy, as there are many still at liberty where she is working, whom she desires to bring together for proper treatment. Dr Davis very kindly gave her some valuable information, and also allowed her to read his latest report, and to take extracts therefrom. We then went rapidly through some of the wards that they might form some idea as to how the patients are treated in the Institute, here and there speaking to some about their souls. We had the pleasure of distributing another thirteen woollen scarves.

On Tuesday last, twenty of the patients were

ROBBEN ISLAND

brought to the mainland, the majority of them returning to their own homes; to-day another six were brought over. They are what are termed " arrested cases."

16th July.—Spoke very solemnly to two young men, who appeared to be much interested. One young fellow who was confined to bed listened very attentively to the Word. Thank God, there is a power in His Word, and if told out faithfully under the guidance of the Holy Spirit, real fruit from it must be the result sooner or later.

I was asked to speak to a convict to-day, who, some time back, in the heat of passion, shot his own wife, but fortunately only wounded her. However, he seems to have awakened up like a man out of a dream, and realizes what he has done. He is very much troubled, broken, and when I saw him he wept much. As far as I can judge, he is really trusting in Christ, confessing Him to others and trying to make amends for his past sin.

23rd July.—One has golden opportunities among these poor lepers. Dear Lucas grows brighter and brighter every day. The Word of God to him is indeed a sweet morsel. He is truly " The hungry soul," of Prov. xxvii. 7. " To whom every bitter thing is sweet." Without exaggeration, his face literally shines whenever we read to him from the Word of God.

24th July.—I was asked to address about thirty young ladies this evening, in a private class at Claremont, with reference to work among the lepers. The weather being very unfavourable, there were

ONE SOWETH, ANOTHER REAPETH

only twenty present, but we had a very profitable evening.

30th July.—Mr R. M'Murdo from America, on his way to Melbourne, is here for a short stay. I was very glad of his company, and can truly say we had a good time among the lepers. Mr M'Murdo, made the most of his opportunity and spoke earnestly to a few individuals who were able to understand English. Such are the men we like to take over. Lucas could scarcely contain his joy as Mr M'Murdo unfolded the Word of God to him; a short word of prayer commending him tenderly and lovingly to the care of God his Father, and we passed on to Botha. A portion of the Word read and commented upon, brought out as usual the calm confidence of his soul in the unfailing Word of God, though for want of eyesight he is unable to read a single verse from Scripture for himself. We spoke to several in No. 1, some of whom were very sorely afflicted. Every now and then, my companion turned to say, " Well ! well ! brother Fish, such a sight, I have never seen before." Lucas was the first leper he had ever seen, and I venture to say that he would travel a long way to find a brighter one. " This is a great work," said Mr M'Murdo ; " it is a world of itself, so to say; the people in America know nothing about it." " No, Mr M'Murdo, and I am afraid they never will, if they depend on our letters for their knowledge." After a little refreshment, we went to Murray's Bay. Mr M'Murdo was absolutely shocked to see the condition of some of the women. One woman, whose husband had come over to see her, was very near the point of decision.

ROBBEN ISLAND

On our return we visited a new meeting at Lakeside, where Mr M'Murdo spoke to a goodly number.

8th August.—The Commissioner sent for us on our arrival, to show us a letter which he had just received from Pretoria, with reference to Polo. The Government has decided to repatriate him to the Belgian Congo.

There was a nice case in No. 5 Ward—a man just about to step over the line. I was sorry that for want of time, I could not remain longer with him.

Poor Fortuin ! He is an awful object of pity, shut up in a room by himself, with another patient to look after him, his bodily condition is almost beyond words. It was not without much effort, that one was able to come near him. After reading a few passages of Scripture and commending him to God in prayer, I left him to the God of all grace, whose he is, I believe. He is stone blind, and could he have seen his dreadful affliction, he must have said with Job of old, perhaps not so much " Mine eyes seeth thee," but rather, " I see myself." " Wherefore I abhor myself " chap xlii., verses 5 and 6.

15th August.—I had the company of Mr W. M'Kenzie from Kaleba to-day. He, like others, was much impressed by his visit. We spoke to a good many of the patients during the day. I found on introducing Polo to Mr M'Kenzie, that he had met him already in Central Africa, in fact, he came from the same Station. So Polo was able to hold a conversation in his own tongue.

Voortuin was very weak but still rational. We had a few words with him. The boy who had been look-

ONE SOWETH, ANOTHER REAPETH

ing after him was now in bed, in the same room. He gave a beautifully clear testimony as to his faith in the Lord Jesus Christ. He told us that before he came to the Island, he was a man full of good works, but since he had been there, he had found out that there is no good in "dead works." He had now given up the latter, has taken Christ for his Saviour and is now satisfied and happy. He had no fear of dying, for God was with him and good to him. He did not even feel the pains in his body; he was only weak.

We had a good time with the women; one of the nurses, a very fine young lady, showed much interest in what we were saying, and I am inclined to believe that God spoke to her.

29th August.—My brother and his wife were over to-day. Poor Voortuin is gone, and I trust to the Better Land. I felt specially helped of the Lord in speaking to Christians. How easy it is to speak, and what joy also to one's own heart when the Holy Spirit has liberty and room to work in us.

I had to labour hard and long with a case in No. 5 Ward; but it was a joy to watch the effect of God's Word knocking away every human prop, one by one; the light of God's Word dispelling the darkness from the human heart and mind, and implanting true light and joy into the soul. I am not sure if another dear soul in No. 1 was not helped to a better understanding of the truth; so on we go, sowing the good seed in the morning, and in the evening withholding not our hand, not knowing which shall prosper. My closing word to-day was with a few sitting in front of No. 1; two of them were dreadfully afflicted, reminding me of Job when " Satan went forth from the presence of the Lord and smote Job with sore boils, from the sole of his foot unto the crown of his head, and he took him a potsherd to scrape himself withal" (Job ii. 7, 8. His wife suggested that he might " curse God and die " (Dutch, *Bless God*). One might recommend the same course to many a poor leper.

September.—It is a beautiful morning; the captain invited me up on the bridge to get the full benefit of a nice fresh breeze from the west.

About half-way over, we passed a motor launch returning from the Island with a doctor who had been called to see the Commissioner, who is dangerously ill. Only a fortnight ago, whilst crossing, I had a long and interesting conversation with him. I found that he had been to Pondoland, and knew people and places known to me there, but there is one bitter regret that I have, namely, that I did not speak more plainly to him about his soul. Oh, for more moral courage when in the presence of such persons!

I met J. B. in his " self-propeller "; he works it very well now. I had a nice word with him, young Petrus Groenewald being present. The latter is becoming terribly disfigured. I have often spoken to him about his soul, but I am afraid he does not yet see his need of a Saviour. I met his mother later in the day with her husband, who had come over to see her; she is also badly disfigured.

Poor Mr L., he is what they call an " arrested case," and might go back to his home at any time, but rather than bring reproach upon his wife and family, he chooses to remain there or get transferred to a leper

ONE SOWETH, ANOTHER REAPETH

Institute on the mainland. How pathetic! Is there any other disease that the human body is liable to, that brings such a stigma?

I met an old Sesuto Chief and his wife on the Island to-day. With his interpreter he had come over to see his son, who was a leper. His interpreter understood a little English, and also Xosa, so I was able to have a nice talk with him. As far as I could gather, he is really trusting in the Lord, for to my surprise, as soon as I began to read and speak to him, he produced his little pocket Sesuto Testament, and turned up the passages. I enquired if the Chief knew the Lord? He said, "No, he was not yet saved, but he is nevertheless a kind chief, and allowed any missionaries to come into his country."

Had a nice little word with Lucas. Dear fellow, he is sometimes lost for words to express his great joy in the Lord. On the way back, I was able to enter into conversation with a very respectable lady who had been over to see her husband, a man previously holding a good position on the mainland. I enquired as to how he had contracted the disease, but of course, she was at a loss to understand the cause. How it finds its way into some families is a mystery. I have known some most respectable families smitten down by this dire disease. I remember well-to-do people in Cape Town, three of whose children died on the Island. I know also of a young lady who was in an advanced stage, both hands and feet gone, before she was taken to the Institute. The parents managed to conceal her for years, but she was at last torn from them, and died a leper. I might tell of quite a number of the "better class," who have become preys to this terrible affliction. We will find if we turn to the Word of God, that this is no exception to what has gone before. We need only to remind ourselves of the great prophet Moses; on withdrawing his hand from his bosom, he found it leprous as snow. The pride of his sister Miriam was rebuked, and she became leprous, "white as snow." I might go on to tell of the mighty man, Naaman the Syrian, Gehazi, King Uzziah, also, who was "a leper unto the day of his death." All these, and many more, prove conclusively that God is no respecter of persons.

26th September.—"Stormy winds, obeying His will," prevented our crossing last week.

The Commissioner with whom I had an interesting conversation a fortnight ago is now in his grave. In speaking to him on that occasion, I made some reference to spiritual things, but I deeply regret that I did not approach him more directly with regard to his own soul. May God make me more alive to my solemn responsibility, touching the perishing around.

Dear J. B. spoke of his conversion again to-day, and of course *God's Way of Salvation* in Dutch, was much in evidence. It is wonderful how richly God has used this little pamphlet.

How easy it becomes, and what joy it affords, to speak of one's *own* conversion. Some believers have no striking experience to tell; for instance, contrast Lydia and the Philippian jailor (Acts xvi).

The two dear fellows in No 5 to whom I spoke a fortnight ago, closed in with God's offer of Salvation

ONE SOWETH, ANOTHER REAPETH

to-day; I am satisfied, that it is no mere surface work. To Him be all the glory.

16th October.—My health has been much impaired of late, so that I have not been able to go very regularly to the Island. I have been over to-day, and felt fairly well until leaving, when I had a sudden attack of my heart. Fortunately, the Superintendent of the Convict Station was near me, and stood by me for a time. For the moment, I wondered if I were going to end my humble service for the Lord right there on Robben Island. However, the Lord willed it otherwise, and I recovered sufficiently to crawl to the end of the jetty; but I was no sooner in the motor launch, than I had another attack, and was practically lifted on to the steamer. For a little while I felt very shaky, but as we came out into the cold wind, I again revived.

Reverting to the Island, I may say, that I had a long talk with Mr M. on "faith healing." He told me that they were expecting a Mr Martin, a Dutch Reformed minister, that week, who claims to have some gift, or confidence in "Faith Healing." On referring to the visit of Mr J. Hickson, a short while ago, and appealing to Mr M. as to the result of his visit. I was immediately met with the question, "Who can say that no blessing resulted from Mr Hickson's visit?" I must admit that a number of patients have been sent from the Island since his visit there; whether this is the result of his mission or not, I cannot say; neither do I think any one can. I saw a number of the patients, and I met one man who only the day before accepted Christ as his Saviour. On the way back in the boat, I had a long conversation with Mr

ROBBEN ISLAND

T., who a little while ago was released from the Island. He has great faith in the Chaulmoogra oil treatment. He told me that shortly after he was brought to the Island, he lost heart and did not much care what became of him; one day he met a friend of his on the Island, who reasoned with him in the following homely way: " Fred, if you were fighting with a man, and he knocked you down, would you not rise and fight him ? " " Yes," he said, " I would." " Just so, you have a malignant disease, and you must fight it." He then took courage, and commenced, first by taking five capsules a day, and increased the number until he reached over sixty per day ; and in addition to this he took hot baths frequently, rubbing his body thoroughly with the oil, immediately after leaving the bath, and he says the result was good.

26th October.—My brother and I, in order to cover more ground, went in different directions. I met a dear believer in No. 1. Oh, so sorely afflicted and tormented by flies ; and no tender hand near to drive them away. It did my heart good, to hear him speak of his confidence in God, and so grateful that any one would condescend to come near him. I said, by way of testing his faith, " Do you really believe that that poor body of yours will one day be transformed into a body of glory, like unto the Lord's ? " " Oh, yes I am certain of it, Sir; God's promises can never fail."

I had a burning desire to go to Murray's Bay ; so after taking a little to eat, and lifting up my heart to God for guidance, I went. Nearing one of the wards, I heard some native women chatting at the back.

ONE SOWETH, ANOTHER REAPETH

At once I felt that was my chance to begin. As I approached them I enquired if they would like me to read something from the Bible in their own language. "Oh, yes," was the reply. I then read several verses from John's Gospel, commenting on the verses as I went on. It was soon evident that they were interested. One dear woman with a beautiful face—her hands and feet bad—wept again and again. Thank God, when hearts are touched by His Word. I am sure that God spoke to those dear women to-day. Just before leaving them, I enquired how they had enjoyed the oranges I sent them the previous week (thirteen paraffine boxes full). "Oh, thank you, Sir, they were very nice." But imagine what one old woman said: "The oranges were very nice, sir, but the words you have been reading are much nicer; the oranges are only for this life, but the Words of God, we shall take to heaven." Really I could have shouted "Hallelujah!" Just before leaving the female location, I spoke to two women who were confined to bed. One has known the Lord for some years; she is bright and full of confidence as to the future; not badly afflicted, but weak. The other may be saved, but needing help regarding her assurance.

CHAPTER XX.

HOME TO ENGLAND ONCE MORE.

For some considerable time my health has not been good. Especially with regard to my nervous system. On more than one occasion whilst on the Island, I have fainted away, and I wondered if I were going to end my humble service for the lepers right there. But God has willed it otherwise, and has so arranged matters, that my dear wife and I have been able to take our passage to England.

I have lately been to the Transvaal on a brief visit, to see some of my old friends. Whilst in Johannesburg, Mr W. Hughes and I arranged to visit the large leper location, situated about six miles outside of Pretoria, and which is surrounded by very extensive, nicely laid out grounds. Some twenty-three years ago, Mr James F. Goch and I visited the same compound, but it has grown considerably since then. There were at that time about 200 inmates in the Hospital; to-day there are no less than 874 poor, wretched lepers. It is enough to move a heart of stone, to go through the different wards. Quite recently 150 have been discharged as arrested cases; so that previously there were over 1000 in the Asylum, which would constitute it the largest leper location in South Africa. Mr Hughes and I were able to speak to quite a number of the patients during our three

HOME TO ENGLAND ONCE MORE

and a half hours' stay. I am sure two women who urged us to enter their little room, were definitely helped with regard to our Lord's Return. A Dutch hymn, a word of prayer, and we moved on. In passing through the location I ran against an old Robben Island patient; poor fellow he was so surprised to meet me, that in a moment of excitement it seemed as if he would have embraced me. His first questions were. Had I come to Pretoria to stay? and would I be able to visit them? On hearing that I was about to leave for England he looked sad, and hoped that I would soon return again, and be able to visit them.

Here is a field for one who could obtain permission from the Government to visit them regularly. It might not be easy for a stranger to gain admittance to the camp, but it is well worth trying for. As far as I am concerned, personally, I should have no difficulty in getting a permit, for the simple reason that I have held one for many years.

The question I should now have to first consider is, whether the great altitude would suit me, at my present time of life.

I am quite sure that the Dutch Reform people are not unmindful of the needs of those poor creatures.

Mr C. Bourgum, connected with the Swiss Mission, visits them once a week, but oh, how little can be done in a few hours among so many, a large number of whom are confined to bed.

May the Lord stir up the hearts of His dear people with regard to this great need.

When about to leave the Superintendent, Dr de

ROBBEN ISLAND

Vos, kindly invited me to the camp for a few days to hold Services among the patients. But I had to decline, on account of other engagements in Johannesburg.

After my return from the Transvaal, on the 7th of March, I made a few visits to the Island to bid the patients farewell.

It was very pathetic to watch how deeply some felt the parting. One dear old Malay wept as I spoke to him of Christ, a very rare thing indeed, for they are not prepared to accept the testimony of Scripture concerning *Him*; how sad! I came across a terrible case in one of the wards to-day, the like of which I have not met with for years. I tried in every way to come near him, but it was impossible, and if the salvation of his soul depended in any way upon my speaking to him that morning, then he must perish. O, the awfulness of such a case! God knows, this is no exaggeration.

Perhaps it would not be out of place to add a few remarks here in regard to our voyage to England.

We left Cape Town on the 14th of April 1924, and had a most enthusiastic send-off at the Docks. About forty Christians from the different Assemblies sang as the boat moved slowly out, those well-known verses: "How good is the God we adore," etc.

Several of the passengers were impressed; one old gentleman, a retired Civil servant, remarked the next day that he "thought it was beautiful." It is impossible to estimate the amount of good which may follow, even from the singing of those two verses.

The captain is an exceedingly nice man, and gave

Leper lunatics with Nurse.

About to lower the remains of the British Ex-Consul of Lobito Bay, who died within a few days after leaving the Harbour.

Our send-off at Cape Town as the s.s. *Adolph Woermann* was leaving the Dock. A large number of Christians are among the crowd.

HOME TO ENGLAND ONCE MORE

me every encouragement to hold Services on board. A fair number came together each Lord's Day to hear the Word, the captain himself being present. One dear lady was definitely brought to the Lord, and openly confessed Him one morning before the captain, saying : " I have got now what I have been longing for, for years, and I am satisfied."

Our voyage has not been altogether an uneventful one.

At Lobeto Bay we took on board the Ex-British Consul of that Port, and within a week we had the painful necessity of committing his body to a watery grave, to await the resurrection. There will be a resurrection " both of the just and the unjust."

The usual custom is to sew up the body in canvas, but in this case a rough coffin was made ; some very choice lilies and ferns, which were highly valued by the chief steward, were cut down to decorate the coffin.

The Burial Service was given entirely into my hands by the captain; consequently I felt a great responsibility devolved upon me; hundreds of passengers stood before me, the captain, doctor and officers being on my right. I told my hearers that the death of our friend immediately affected his widow and family. The death of a king, not only affects the members of that royal family, but the entire empire over which he had reigned, and often means a very radical change. But the death of the Son of God, utterly surpasses all others, bringing about eternal and wide-world results.

A great monarch dies and is immediately succeeded by the next heir to the throne. But the Son of God died, and was again raised to sit upon the Throne of

ROBBEN ISLAND

Thrones. What a glorious triumph over death and the grave! Subsequently on our arrival at Southampton, we met a brother of the departed one, a fine gentleman, who had come to glean any information he could, regarding his brother's sad end. How the human heart seeks for comfort; the Christian knows where it is to be found, for his God is " The Father of Mercies, and the God of *all* comfort."

This, dear reader, is but a greatly abbreviated account of visits paid to those poor stricken lepers, during our thirty-four years of service in South Africa. God has abundantly blessed the effort, setting His seal thereto in the salvation of many of their souls.

Numbers of His own have been cheered, helped and blessed through His Word. To Him be all the glory.

Will you petition "the Lord of the Harvest," that the work may continue amongst those needy ones? And that He will raise up, send forth and sustain the men whom He has so called and equipped, for His own service among the lepers.